A Songwriter's Guide

MUSIC PUBLISHING

REVISED EDITION

RANDY POE

WRITER'S DIGEST BOOKS
CINCINNATI, OHIO

Music Publishing: A Songwriter's Guide. Copyright © 1997 by Randy Poe. Printed and bound in the United States of America. All rights reserved. No part of this book may be reproduced in any form or by any electronic or mechanical means including information storage and retrieval systems without permission in writing from the publisher, except by a reviewer, who may quote brief passages in a review. Published by Writer's Digest Books, an imprint of F&W Publications, Inc., 1507 Dana Avenue, Cincinnati, Ohio 45207. (800) 289-0963. Second edition.

Other fine Writer's Digest Books are available from your local bookstore or direct from the publisher.

06   05   04   03   02   7   6   5   4   3

Library of Congress Cataloging-in-Publication Data

Poe, Randy.
    Music publishing : a songwriter's guide / Randy Poe.—2nd ed.
       p.   cm.
    Includes index.
    ISBN 0-89879-754-3 (alk. paper)
    1. Popular music—Writing and publishing.   I.   Title.
MT67.P75   1997   97-25566
070.5'794—dc21   CIP
                                                                                        MN

Edited by Julie Wesling Whaley
Production edited by Patrick G. Souhan
Designed by Clare Finney

ACKNOWLEDGMENTS

I couldn't have written the first or second editions of this book without the input of a number of people. Many thanks go to the following: Robin Ahrold, Connie Ambrosch, Ed Arrow, Lew Bachman, Pat Baird, Marilyn Bergman, Del Bryant, Steve Day, Roger Deitz, Bob Fead, Arlene Fishbach, Gary Ford, Dr. Betty Gipson, the late Morton Gould, Peter Guralnick, Rupert Holmes, Dave Jasen, Michael Kerker, Bob Leone, the late Lou Levy, Irv Lichtman, Helen Mallory, Tom McCaffrey, Frank Military, Linda Newmark, Norman Odlum, the late Bill Poe, Marjorie Poe, the late Doc Pomus, Frances W. Preston, Gary Roth, Rick Sanjek, Jerry Schilling, Joan Schulman, Karen Sherry, Alison Smith, Greg Sowders, Jim Steinblatt, Jane Stevens, William Velez, Cynthia Weil, Bobby Weinstein, George David Weiss, Terry Woodford, Graham Woolwine, Gene Yasuda, Kayoko Yasuda, George Young, Linda Young, and everyone else who has given me advice and encouragement regarding this book over the last decade.

Thanks and "high fives" to Jerry Leiber and Mike Stoller. It's been a special thrill to be able to hang out with my childhood heroes on an almost daily basis for more than a dozen years now.

Very special thanks and lots of love to my wife, Mina, and to my son, Riley. Mother and child have been very patient and understanding during my frequent late nights at the computer.

Thanks once again to Julie Wesling Whaley, who went above and beyond the call of duty by editing both the first and second editions of this book. I truly couldn't have done it without her either time.

Finally, I have discovered that the older I get, the more I have to accept the loss of some wonderful people in my life. Upon finishing the manuscript for the first edition of this book, I was lucky enough to have the great lyricist, Sammy Cahn, offer to write the foreword. I first met Sammy in 1981, and learned from him the true meaning of the phrase "class act." His passing in 1993 was a blow from which I have yet to recover. There will never be another like him.

For Mina and Riley

Foreword

When Randy Poe, who is almost like a son to me, called and asked if I would write a foreword to a book he had written, I was more than happy to oblige. Music publishing is a unique and fascinating part of what words and music are all about. I have vivid and lasting memories of music publishers. For instance, one of the very first music publishers I ever met was a gentleman called Joe Davis. His office was in the Roseland building—the famed Roseland of the Dime-a-Dance Ballroom. Joe Davis's office couldn't have been more than two tiny rooms. On the wall there was a sign that I can still see. It simply said, "A contract a day keeps the landlord away!" I am sure it did then and I am sure that it does today.

From the Roseland building, I next encountered the DeSylva, Brown & Henderson building on the northeast corner of 49th Street. An amazing number of publishing companies filled this building, and on a hot New York day, before air conditioning, with all the windows open, you could hear the din of all the Tonk pianos going at the same time. (I often wonder if the phrase "Honky-Tonk" comes from the piano of the name?)

As time went on, the publishers moved from the east corner of 49th Street to the now famed Brill Building on the northwest corner of 49th and Broadway. In time came Radio City, and again the publishers moved.

So, now that you know about where they came from, what about them? Well, the publishers I used to know were all the most marvelous and wonderful and colorful people. The songwriters I knew then were (well, most of them) naive and romantic and totally involved with creating words and music—totally *un*involved with the "business" behind the management of their songs. This was "the publisher's domain."

And it was a joyful and rewarding business, especially when you came up with a "hit" for the publisher. The songwriter then (and maybe now as well) signed whatever contract was placed before him. He was so happy about having a publisher "take" his song, he didn't stop to think that maybe he was being "taken" as well.

The early contracts between a writer and his publisher were seemingly rather simple, but they often contained many traps in the "small print" that benefitted the publisher. It was only after The Songwriters Guild came along that many of the injustices were eliminated (see p. 82).

This book is an absolute guide to avoiding such problems, a guide to the proper procedures for signing a music publishing contract, and for understanding what the terms of that contract should be. Unfortunately, the neophyte writer is seldom in a position to ask for or to dictate any terms. But, assuming the publisher really wants your song, then you are in an enviable position—providing you understand the terms you should be asking for. This book explains those terms to you. I really wish there was such a guide book around when I started.

Finally, your first concern should be the writing. But, having written, read this book. You will find it invaluable!

Sammy Cahn, New York City, May 2, 1990.

Contents

Introduction

You have been pounding the pavement for ages. You've sent tapes of your songs to dozens of music publishers. You've set up appointments with publishers who have listened to your songs while you fidgeted nervously in an uncomfortable chair.

The tapes that you've sent in the mail have come back either unopened or with rejection slips. The publishers you have actually met with have all politely turned down your material.

But you have hounded the secretary of the professional manager of a very important music publishing company for weeks. You've called so many times that she has even mentioned your name to her boss.

One day while the secretary is out to lunch, the professional manager answers your call himself. He almost never makes appointments to listen to material by songwriters he doesn't know. But it's Friday, he's just gotten his paycheck, he's in a great mood and Monday seems like it's a year away. So he agrees to see you and listen to your tape Monday morning at ten o'clock sharp. Besides, he's sure he's heard your name somewhere. You might be someone he can't afford to ignore.

Having achieved this major victory you spend the weekend picking exactly which three songs you want him to hear. You're so excited, it's almost impossible to sleep Sunday night.

For years you have dreamed of seeing your name in parentheses just below the title of your song on a record by your favorite artist—or any artist for that matter. In a few hours you'll be meeting with the person who can help turn that dream into a reality.

Monday morning at 9:58 A.M. you arrive at the publishing company's office and finally meet that secretary you have spoken to a hundred times. She ushers you into the professional manager's office.

He's on the phone, but he smiles and motions for you to have a seat. The chair is extremely comfortable. He's talking and laughing with whoever is on the other end of the line. He is obviously in a very good mood. You're beginning to feel relaxed and at home.

He hangs up the phone, extends his hand, introduces himself as Bob and says, "Let's hear these songs of yours."

You give him your tape. He puts it in his tape player, and your song demo comes floating out through the giant speakers of his two thousand dollar sound system. Bob smiles. You smile. For some reason your song sounds better to you than it ever has before—and it's not because of those expensive speakers. The melody flows, the lyrics are almost poetic and the hook is so good that the secretary sticks her head in the door, smiles at her boss and gives you an approving nod.

By the second verse you can hear Bob tapping his foot to the rhythm. When the hook comes around this time he's actually singing along!

Bob listens to the song all the way through to the end. When it's over, he has a look of amazement on his face.

The entire scene is repeated as he listens to the second song, and then to the third one. He asks if you have any other songs with you. Of course you do.

As he begins listening to the next tape, you realize that no publisher has ever listened beyond your first three songs before. In fact, at other meetings, most of your time was spent watching the publisher's back as he fast-forwarded your tape from one song to the next, listening only to the first few lines of each song before stopping the tape and handing it back to you with a polite "No thanks."

Suddenly you're back in the present. Bob has just listened to the last song you brought with you. He begins to talk excitedly about an exclusive. You become confused. He's still smiling as he politely explains that copublishing would be out of the question for now, but that he will fight for a strong advance.

You are hearing terms you've never heard of before. Bob seems to be speaking in a foreign language. You've never suffered from claustrophobia in your life, but as he begins talking about synchs and mechanicals you start to feel that the walls of Bob's office are closing in around you.

He talks about numbers and percentages, he mentions something about a guy named Harry Fox, and then suddenly he's asking if you're BMI or ASCAP. He seems to really expect you to know what he's talking about.

You're ready to bolt for the nearest door or window. As you're trying to remember what floor you're on, your eyes sweep across the room in search of any exit. On one wall you see a bookshelf. The title of one of the books seems to jump out at you—*Music Publishing: A Songwriter's Guide.*

Slowly you calm down. The smile returns to your face. You turn back to Bob and say, "I'm really glad that you like my songs and I appreciate the offer you're making. But first I'll need a few days to consider everything we've discussed."

The book you need to read to understand the ins and outs of music publishing is in your hands. All you have to do is turn the page.

One
MUSIC PUBLISHING YESTERDAY AND TODAY

*M*usic publishing is an industry that is constantly evolving. From the origins of Tin Pan Alley in the late 1800s to the conglomerate craze of the 1980s and 1990s, music publishing has gone through numerous changes for a variety of reasons.

It is conceivable that one could become involved with music publishing today and learn all of the current technicalities of the business without knowing or being concerned about its history. However, I believe it's important to learn how the basic principles of music publishing evolved from the need to establish ownership of songs and collect income from them. And how, despite all of the technological changes over the last hundred years or so—as well as major changes in copyright law—the business of music publishing remains what it has always been: the ownership, promotion and administration of songs.

To prevent this from becoming a history textbook, though, rather than going all the way back to the day Johann Gutenberg began toying with the idea of movable type, let's start at the beginning of the modern era of music publishing in America.

PRE-TIN PAN ALLEY

Like most other successful American enterprises, the music publishing industry in the United States was spawned by entrepreneurship. Before New York City became music publishing's headquarters in the late 1800s, there were small entrepreneurial music publishers all around the country.

These pioneers didn't necessarily make a career just from publishing music. Neither was it necessarily their foremost activity. In many cases the early music publisher was simply a person who owned a printing press.

Along with printing books, posters, stationery and advertisements, the town printer would, on occasion, be asked by a local musician to print sheet music copies of his or her latest composition.

In his capacity as a music publisher, the printer would sometimes make a deal with the composer regarding the terms by which the composer and the publisher

The printer would sometimes make a deal with the composer. These early agreements later evolved into the modern-day song contract.

would share royalties on copies sold. These early agreements later evolved into the modern-day song contract.

If the printer/music publisher was also a stationer (which was often the case), he usually sold copies of the sheet music in his stationery store. The sheet music would also be sold at the local music store if one existed.

To reach beyond the city limits, the printer/publisher frequently hired traveling salesmen to sell the sheet music throughout a particular region on a commission basis. Along with the clothes and household supplies the salesman usually carried on his rounds, he now included a case of sheet music samples as an important part of his product line.

When the traveling salesman came to town, he would sell clothes to the local clothing stores, household supplies to the general store or notions shop, and sheet music to the town's music store or the local "five and dime." The more talented of these salesmen would actually play the songs they had in their cases of sheet music samples to convince the proprietor of a store to order copies of the sheet music. This early concept of promoting songs later became an extremely important part of the music publishing business.

Among these salesmen there were a few who felt there was a growing future in music publishing. These early entrepreneurs—familiar by now with what music was most popular in a particular region—established their own publishing companies.

Some wrote and published their own songs. Some acquired new songs from the songwriters whose sheet music they had previously sold on behalf of other publishers. Others began looking for new songwriters to sign to publishing agreements.

Next, it was only a matter of paying a printer to print their sheet music or, for the braver of this new breed, of acquiring printing presses so that the entire operation became an in-house affair. At this point, America was just a beat away from Tin Pan Alley.

TIN PAN ALLEY

A combination of several events brought about the creation of Tin Pan Alley in New York City during the late 1800s, the foremost of which was improved and cheaper transportation.

By the middle of 1869, America's first transcontinental railway route had been completed. Over the next two decades, tens of thousands of miles of railroad tracks were laid in place.

With access to most of the country's major cities easily available, groups of entertainers originating from New York City now traveled all across the country performing their acts in theaters and music halls.

The entertainers in question were singers, dancers and comedians who traveled and performed together throughout the country. This traveling variety show was a form of entertainment called vaudeville. Among the legends of show business who were a part of the vaudeville world were the Marx Brothers, Fred Astaire, W.C. Fields and the Four Cohans—a family of performers that included a boy named George M. Thanks to vaudeville, the music publishers had a constant source of performers in need of new material to take on the road.

HOW TIN PAN ALLEY GOT ITS NAME

As the story goes, a *New York Herald* reporter named Monroe Rosenfeld was assigned to write about the new music publishing industry that had settled in Manhattan. To gather information for his story, Rosenfeld went to Harry Von Tilzer Music Publishing Company in the heart of the publishing district. As he exited the building, Rosenfeld heard the pianos being played at all of the publishing firms along Twenty-eighth Street. Since this was before the days of air conditioners, windows were open all along the block. In some of the offices there were composers banging out new melodies, while in other offices the composer and lyricist together would be demonstrating a new song to a vaudeville performer looking for new material. Rosenfeld later reported that the resultant sound on the street was similar to that of tin pans banging against each other. Although Monroe Rosenfeld didn't actually use the phrase "Tin Pan Alley" in his *New York Herald* piece, he did refer to Twenty-eighth Street between Sixth Avenue and Broadway as the "Alley"—and, as a result, Tin Pan Alley became the new name of the area where publishing houses were clustered together in New York City.

In New York City the theaters, booking agents and the *New York Clipper*—the industry trade paper—were located around Twenty-eighth Street. Since this was the area where the entertainers of the era were hanging out, and since those entertainers frequently traveled around the country performing songs before large audiences of prospective sheet music buyers, it made good sense for the music publishers to be in this neighborhood so that the entertainers were easily accessible.

Near the end of the nineteenth century, everything seemed to fall into place on and around Twenty-eighth Street—the area of New York known as Tin Pan Alley. Among the important music publishing companies that made up Tin Pan Alley at the time were the firms of M. Witmark & Sons; F.A. Mills; Leo. Feist, Inc.; Harry Von Tilzer Music Publishing Company; and Jerome H. Remick & Company. Several of these firms were originated by the salesmen-turned-publishers mentioned earlier.

The general setup of these music publishing companies in Tin Pan Alley days was relatively simple. The company had an office that—depending on the size of the operation—had one or more rooms, each containing a piano. The publisher would then hire songwriters to sit in each room during the day and create new songs.

Competition among the publishers was fierce. Songs were needed on a constant basis. Up and down Twenty-eighth Street, composers sat and banged out new melodies, while lyricists stood by trying to come up with catchy phrases to fit their partners' tunes. It is said that this cacophony of pianos, which could be heard all around the block, caused the music publishing community to acquire the nickname of "Tin Pan Alley."

The more talented salesmen would actually play the songs they had in their cases of sheet music. This early concept of promoting songs later became an extremely important part of the music publishing business.

Tin Pan Alley (West Twenty-eighth Street) at the turn of the twentieth century: the industry trade paper, the New York Clipper; *music publisher Jerome H. Remick & Company; and the William Morris talent agency. (Photo courtesy of ASCAP archives)*

Once the Tin Pan Alley songwriter or songwriting team had finished a new song, it was the publisher's job to go out and persuade an entertainer to add the number to his or her act. This process, which originated with the Tin Pan Alley publishing companies, became known as song plugging.

An example of the lengths some song pluggers would go to involves legendary music publisher Lou Levy. In 1936 Lou was managing the young songwriting team of Sammy Cahn and Saul Chaplin who had written a song called "Shoe Shine

Boy." "The building at 729 Seventh Avenue was filled with talent agencies and music companies," Lou recalls. "I gave the elevator operator fifty cents a day to sing 'Shoe Shine Boy' as he went up and down in the car. His passengers would ask him about it and he'd say, 'Oh, that song is gonna be a big hit. You ought to get onto it right away.' "

For many of the publishers who had begun as salesmen, it seemed only natural that once the "product" was created, every effort should be made to see that it was "sold." Since song plugging was a new concept, there were no ground rules. Whether the plugger was the publisher himself or a hired hand capable of singing, playing or whistling a tune, the only rule was to go out and persuade someone—the more well-known the better—to sing the song the song plugger was plugging.

After an entertainer agreed to perform the number, the publisher would print sheet music of the song, often with a picture of the performer on the cover. This was done to appeal to the entertainer's ego as well as to get the performer to keep the number in his act. The sheet music would then be distributed to wholesalers, or "jobbers," throughout the country, in preparation for the orders that would, hopefully, begin pouring in from the retailers.

The performer—along with his or her fellow vaudeville acts—would then go "on the road" via the now elaborate passenger train system, singing the song at the music halls and theaters of the vaudeville circuit into which he or she had been booked by one of the agencies located on or near Twenty-eighth Street.

Frequently, the day after the popular singer had performed in a particular town, the local music store (and other stores of the day that carried sheet music) would be flooded with requests for copies of the new song that had been sung the night before. Because pianos had become one of the main sources of entertainment in the home during the 1800s, sheet music was much in demand. It was the number of copies of sheet music sold that determined whether or not the song was a "hit."

The combination of events that brought about the creation and success of Tin Pan Alley, then, were: the improved railway system; the creation and popularity of vaudeville; the popularity of pianos as a major source of entertainment in the American home; the proximity of the various facets of the entertainment industry in New York City; and the new concepts of how music publishing companies should operate, as devised by the men and women who made Tin Pan Alley run.

These new concepts were: to hire songwriters to create new songs in the popular style of the moment; to plug, or promote, the songs by persuading performers to add the numbers to their acts; and to market the songs in sheet music form that frequently featured the performer on the cover.

The result of all of these factors was a remarkable leap in sheet music sales and, consequently, an equally remarkable leap in profits for the music publishers.

By the end of the first decade of the twentieth century, millions of copies of sheet music had been sold. Some of the most popular songs of the decade are purported to have sold as many as a million copies *each*.

THE ARRIVAL OF RECORDINGS, RADIOS AND FILMS WITH SOUND

New technology of the early twentieth century had a profound effect on music publishing. At first the effect was potentially devastating because the U.S. Copyright

Act, on which the principles of publishing are based, failed to keep up with the country's rapid technological growth.

Prior to the U.S. Copyright Act of 1909, there was much confusion about what monies might be owed to publishers by manufacturers of piano rolls. After the law was enacted, the publisher received two cents for each of his songs that appeared on a piano roll or recording manufactured by these rapidly expanding American industries.

Beginning in the 1920s, both recordings and radio had become important new forms of home entertainment, and many of the vaudeville performers had quickly become radio stars.

Publishers believed if they could get the stars of this new medium to perform their songs on the radio, sheet music sales were bound to skyrocket. If these stars also made recordings of the songs, then additional profits would be made from record sales.

Before the decade of the 1920s was over, another major technological breakthrough arrived that caused substantial changes in the world of Tin Pan Alley. This latest breakthrough was the addition of sound to film.

On October 6, 1927, the first movie musical opened. Entitled *The Jazz Singer* and starring Al Jolson, the film was the first to incorporate songs and moving images on the big screen. *The Jazz Singer* was a box office smash, prompting Hollywood to turn to Broadway and vice versa.

Former stars of vaudeville and Broadway were soon on their way to California, along with the songwriters who were now in demand by the Hollywood studios. In need of older songs as well as new ones, motion picture companies such as Warner Bros. began to purchase entire publishing companies from their original owners.

Sound recordings became prominent after World War II, and sheet music became a less important part of the industry. In fact, by the early 1950s, many publishers had begun to "job out" the printing portion of their operation to companies who specialized in printing sheet music, song folios, and band, orchestra and choral arrangements for many different copyright-owning publishers.

This practice has led to today's "print publishers," who sometimes own few or no copyrights of their own. Their business is simply to print and distribute music on behalf of the copyright-holding publishers who share in the income earned from print sales. Today very few music publishers still have their own print divisions. The print business—although still important—is now a much smaller aspect of the overall industry. It wouldn't be profitable for any but the wealthiest of publishing companies to maintain an in-house print operation.

ELVIS PRESLEY AND THE BIRTH OF ROCK & ROLL

With the advent of television came the variety show. When Elvis Presley appeared on the *Dorsey Brothers Show*, the *Milton Berle Show*, the *Steve Allen Show*, and finally, the *Ed Sullivan Show* during 1956, he not only drove millions of American teenagers wild, he also put panic in the hearts of the older music publishers.

In a few brief TV appearances he showed America that popular music had a new name, a new audience and a new attitude. Simultaneously, he proved that

Songwriting team Mike Stoller and Jerry Leiber with Elvis Presley. In the early Rock & Roll era (pre-Beatles), recording artists rarely wrote their own material. They relied on songwriters and music publishers for a steady supply of hit songs. (Photo courtesy of Leiber & Stoller)

television—for better or for worse—would become the ultimate entertainment medium of the second half of the twentieth century.

From this point on, the music publishing industry would either cater to a youthful audience, rest on its laurels and wait for this "latest phenomenon" to blow over, turn its emphasis toward Broadway shows, or head off to Hollywood to be a part of the last years of the big-budget movie musicals.

Those who chose to wait out the "fad" are either still waiting or eventually took on an "if you can't beat 'em, join 'em" attitude. Those who took the last train to Hollywood must have been shocked when Elvis and other teen idols rode into town too, taking over the once sacred Hollywood musical.

This new musical would now emphasize a score by Rock & Roll songwriting teams such as Jerry Leiber and Mike Stoller or Doc Pomus and Mort Shuman or by others who—along with these writers—had helped to create Rock & Roll. On occasion, older songwriters who were capable of adapting to this new style of music began composing for the new Hollywood musical as well.

Adaptability, in fact, quickly became the operative word in the music industry. New York was still filled with music publishers, including many new ones who specialized in Rock & Roll. But the writers who had been such an important part of Tin Pan Alley were now either writing almost solely for Broadway and films or had been replaced by teenagers and young adults whose songs were saying what young audiences wanted to hear. Very few songwriters of Tin Pan Alley's heyday were able to (or desired to) make the transition to Rock & Roll.

By the early 1960s, the music publishing industry had caught on to the youthful crazes that were sweeping the country. If Chubby Checker turned young people on to "The Twist," publishers responded with new songs about the popular dance, or at least with new songs that could be "twisted to." Meanwhile, Hollywood was quick to base entire, mostly low-budget movies on the dance craze of the moment.

Many publishers wisely moved into the recording industry, signing acts to record the songs written by the publishing division's staff writers. These independent record/publishing companies now had the best of both worlds. Everything seemed to be working out well for the American music publishing industry until yet another act appeared on the *Ed Sullivan Show.*

Many publishers moved into the recording industry, signing acts to record the songs written by the publishing division's staff writers.

ENTER THE BEATLES

On February 9, 1964, the Beatles took the country by storm when they appeared on Ed Sullivan's Sunday night variety show, sparking what the press would soon dub "the British invasion."

Along with their unique sound, haircuts and clothing, the Beatles brought along something American publishers weren't yet prepared to deal with: their own self-penned songs. At least Elvis Presley still needed writers!

But suddenly, in the mid-1960s, the world of popular music seemed to be filled with acts who supplied their own material. After all the adapting they had done over the past decade, how were publishers supposed to cope with this new wrinkle?

At first the solution was simple. Many publishers were able to convince these self-contained acts that it was still necessary to sign over 100 percent of what is commonly known as the "publisher's share" of their songs to an "established" publisher who could properly promote and administer the compositions. (The concepts of publisher's share/songwriter's share are explained in chapter six.)

Singer/songwriter Rupert Holmes, whose hits as a recording artist include the number one record "Escape (The Piña Colada Song)," says that publishers suddenly became very interested in him when he signed a recording contract with a major label. "A transition had taken place in the music industry, which was that publishers were finding that they no longer knew how to get songs recorded because there were not a lot of artists recording outside material—certainly not a lot of artists recording the kind of traditional pop songs that people would sit down and write in the Brill Building.*

"The publishers said, 'How are we going to get songs recorded when artists are recording their own songs?' So they decided, 'We'll turn it inside out. We won't place the songs. We'll sign the artists who have recording contracts and get their publishing. That guarantees us ten songs on every album they make.' "

When Rupert became a recording artist he received a very large advance from a major publisher "with a stipulation that I would record ten songs every year. It was their way of placing ten songs on an album—just the opposite of how publishers had been doing business for decades."

---

*The Brill Building—1619 Broadway in New York City—was once filled with publishers of Broadway shows and traditional pop songs—publishers of the old Tin Pan Alley variety. During the late 1950s and early 1960s, more modern publishers and a few independent record companies moved in. At that time the Brill Building became the place where such writers as Jerry Leiber, Mike Stoller, Neil Diamond, Doc Pomus, Mort Shuman, Ellie Greenwich and Jeff Barry created many of their pop classics. Contrary to popular belief, however, the Brill Building was *not* the spot where Carole King, Gerry Goffin, Neil Sedaka, Howie Greenfield, Barry Mann and Cynthia Weil wrote some of their biggest hits. Their publishers were actually in a building across the street and up the block at 1650 Broadway.

RUPERT HOLMES

On several occasions throughout this book I have quoted Rupert Holmes's thoughts on a variety of topics. I felt Rupert was a most fitting songwriter to call upon since he has achieved success in practically every area of the music business. He is a composer, lyricist, author, international performing and recording artist, arranger and record producer. If I were a young songwriter, my goal would be to try to have a career as diverse and successful as his.

As a songwriter/performer he has appeared on the *Billboard* pop charts on several occasions, including a three-week stay at number one with the single "Escape (The Piña Colada Song)." He also received gold records in the United States, Canada, Japan and Australia for his album *Partners in Crime.*

As a songwriter/producer he has been responsible for albums by Barbra Streisand and others, as well as the Jets' platinum single "You Got It All."

His Broadway work includes the creation of the book, music, lyrics and orchestrations for "The Mystery of Edwin Drood," a musical that won five Tony awards, including Best Broadway Musical of 1986.

Along with Barbra Streisand and the Jets, Rupert's songs have been recorded by Dolly Parton, Dionne Warwick, Barry Manilow, Judy Collins, Rita Coolidge, Mac Davis, Manhattan Transfer, and many others.

During the 1990s, Rupert's popularity and longevity were once again confirmed when many of his older albums were reissued on compact disc for the first time, including his 1974 debut solo album, the cult classic *Widescreen.*

Rupert Holmes's credits are impressive, but they didn't come overnight. It can truly be said that he has paid his dues. In his own words, "I said 'yes' to everything anyone in this business asked me to do. There was no job too small."

In his career Rupert has been signed to every type of contract I discuss in chapter six, and today he has his own very successful publishing company. His comments are based on many years of experience in the music business. Whether you are a beginning songwriter or have already made songwriting your career, it might be a good idea to absorb what Rupert has to say.

Because of such industry practices, many well-known acts of the era signed away the publisher's share to publishers who needed to do little more than sit back and watch the money roll in from the record companies and other sources.

Before long, many of the self-contained acts (whether they were bands whose members wrote the material they recorded or were simply solo singer/songwriters) began to realize the importance of publishing. With the help of entertainment attorneys and better-informed managers, it soon became commonplace for a self-contained act to set up an in-house publishing company.

These in-house publishing companies generally consisted of songs written and recorded by the band or singer/songwriter. Therefore, when records were sold, rather than paying the publishing royalties to an outside publisher, the record company paid those royalties to the publishing company owned by the self-contained act.

Of course, the record company executives weren't fools. They were aware that many of the jobs that once rested on the publisher's shoulders had now become the record company's responsibility. In the Tin Pan Alley days, when sheet music was the tangible product preferred by the public, it was the publishing company's job to print, distribute and promote that product. When recordings took over as the preferred form of musical entertainment in the home after World War II, it became the record company's responsibility to press, distribute and promote.

Based on this turn of events, in many cases (especially prior to the onset of the 1980s), if a self-contained act wanted to sign a recording contract with a particular label, the act also had to sign a publishing agreement with the label's own in-house publishing company. It was in this manner that many record companies became owners of important publishing catalogs containing some of the most valuable Rock & Roll songs of the 1950s, 1960s and 1970s.

Although similar deals continue to be made today, they are much less frequent. In fact, when a label demands that publishing be incorporated into a recording contract, it is usually for only a percentage of the publishing as opposed to all of it.

When sheet music was the product preferred by the public, it was the publishing company's job to print, distribute and promote that product. When recordings took over as the preferred form of musical entertainment, it became the record company's responsibility to press, distribute and promote.

MUSIC PUBLISHING TODAY

There is still a thriving music publishing industry in New York City. California's publishing community has continued to grow as well. But the remnants of Tin Pan Alley—that is, publishers who have staff songwriters and who take their songs to artists in a daily attempt to get their songs recorded—have, for the most part, moved south.

Music Row in Nashville, Tennessee, is the current home of the Tin Pan Alley type of publisher. In fact, there is now an annual songwriters' event in Nashville called "Tin Pan South." For songwriters who specialize in Country songs, Nashville is the place to be, just as Twenty-eighth Street in New York City was once the place to be for the pop songwriter.

There are other publishing and recording centers: Seattle; Minneapolis; Chicago; Memphis; Philadelphia; Boston; Muscle Shoals, Alabama; Athens, Georgia; and Jackson, Mississippi have all become centers of various kinds of American music. There are, in fact, many regions throughout the country where publishers can be found.

Today's music publishers have a new attitude about the role they play in the music industry. In many cases the emphasis has begun to lean more and more toward development deals. Rather than simply sign a songwriter and hope that he or she will create something the publisher can convince someone else to record, many publishers now look for that singer/songwriter or self-contained band who the publisher can take into the studio.

What the music publisher hopes to come away with is a high-quality demo (or even a finished master recording) that can then be shopped around to the major record labels. In exchange for footing the bill for the demo production costs, the publisher ends up with all or part of the publishing rights to the songs written by the act for whom the publisher has helped secure a recording contract.

For the nonperforming songwriter there continue to be many non-songwriting performers who constantly need new songs. This is something publishers everywhere are still aware of and are actively pursuing—especially in Nashville. However, to say that a talented nonperforming songwriter has exactly the same chance of success as an equally talented singer/songwriter might not be as accurate a statement as the nonperforming writer would wish.

By becoming involved in producing self-contained acts, many music publishers have continued to be flexible enough to remain an active part of the industry, even though the music business has gone through numerous changes over the decades.

Buying and Selling

In recent years, some music publishers have begun to take advantage of a couple of other available options: buying in and selling out.

At one time the world of music publishing was an industry of several dozen major companies, each of which owned several thousand copyrights, as well as hundreds of smaller companies, each of which owned anywhere from one to several hundred copyrights. As I mentioned earlier, when the Hollywood movie industry began to use songs in films, many of the motion picture companies bought up publishing companies already in existence as a simple way of acquiring a large number of readily available songs.

Since that time, the number of publishing companies has grown and shrunk like an accordion. While new companies are constantly being formed, new and old companies alike are also being bought and incorporated into larger companies. In the last few years there has been an unprecedented amount of buying and selling among music publishers.

Perhaps the most publicized of these various acquisitions was Michael Jackson's purchase of ATV Music Publishing. ATV is a catalog which consists of, among other things, over 250 songs written by the Beatles. Jackson bought ATV for $48 million in 1985. He then turned over the administration* of this valuable company to CBS Songs.

Realizing the increased value of CBS, music industry veterans Charles Koppelman and Martin Bandier, along with New York-based financier Stephen Swid, purchased all of the copyrights owned by CBS Inc. (as well as acquiring administration rights to those songs being administered by the company) in 1986 at a reported cost of $125 million, forming a publishing company called SBK Entertainment World.

The following year, Warner Communications bought the publishing firm of Chappell & Co. for approximately $250 million, merging Warner Bros. Music and Chappell & Co. into a company called Warner/Chappell Music.

In 1989, CBS, now owned by Sony, got back into music publishing (remember, they had previously sold their publishing companies to Koppelman, Bandier and Swid) by purchasing Tree International, a Nashville-based publishing company, for around $40 million. Initially, this new company was called Sony-Tree, but was later changed to simply Sony Music Publishing.

See p. 93 for an in-depth explanation of "administration."

A few days after CBS acquired Tree, SBK Entertainment World was purchased by Thorn-EMI for just over $300 million.

For those who thought Koppelman and his partners were making a mistake when they paid more than a $100 million for the CBS publishing companies in 1986, a little math will show that the trio had the proper profit-making philosophy all along: Buy high, sell higher.

But the story doesn't end there. In 1995, a decade after his purchase of ATV, Michael Jackson merged ATV Music Publishing with Sony Music Publishing, creating the third largest publishing company in the world (at least, until the next mega-merger takes place).

The big question regarding all of these sales, buyouts, acquisitions and mergers is, what happens to all of those songs and all of those songwriters who are caught up in these transactions? For example, if you wrote a song that was signed to a publishing company, only to discover that the company you're signed to is being sold to a giant company tomorrow, and that *that* company is being bought by a huge conglomerate next week, then what are the chances of your song receiving proper attention from that huge conglomerate, which will have literally a million other songs to oversee? This is the reality of music publishing today.

Rupert Holmes expresses his view on merger mania: "When you're working for a public corporation and you're accountable not only to bosses but also to stockholders, you feel you have to make moves that you can defend on paper. In other words, it isn't so stupid to buy the catalog of a famous songwriter who is now dead. It's a wise investment because it's not that speculative. It's a sound move. The trouble is that sound moves generally: 1) are unexciting; 2) don't change anything in the world; and, 3) often end up being exactly that—sound and boring. That's why I equate a lot of publishers with investment bankers."

And what about a songwriter who is signed to a major publisher with hundreds of thousands of songs. "You're a speck in the cosmos," says Rupert. "There's no way that they can be aware of you. They're not going to call you up at three in the morning with a bright idea about how they can get your song placed.

"If 80 percent of the world's publishing is owned by a couple of companies, how are they going to be really excited about you? How can they go to a stockholders' meeting and explain about this incredible new songwriter they found in Brooklyn who shows a lot of promise and has found a way to rhyme 'orange?' It's not going to be on their list of priorities."

A great song is a great song. It will be up to you to write that great song, learn what the music business is all about, make the proper contacts along the way and be in the right place at the right time.

In the end, a great song is a great song. It will be up to you, whether you're a performing songwriter or not, to write that great song, to learn what the music business is all about, to make the proper contacts along the way and to be in the right place at the right time. You will also have to be extremely lucky.

SUMMARY

In this chapter we have covered over a century of music publishing in America. Yesterday the industry was supported by sheet music. Today the sources of income for music publishers are numerous and diverse.

Throughout the intervening decades, copyright laws and technological improvements have changed dramatically, but the function of music publishing has remained constant: the ownership, promotion, and administration of songs.

Two
MUSIC PUBLISHING AND COPYRIGHT LAW

*U*nderstanding what music publishing is first requires an understanding of what copyright is all about. The terms "copyright" and "music publishing" go hand in hand. They don't mean the same thing, but each requires the other in the context of our discussion.

Like a hot dog and a hot dog bun, they are two separate entities, both of which can be "digested" separately. When you put the two together, however, they can be better appreciated.

DEFINITIONS OF "COPYRIGHT" AND "PUBLICATION"

Taken at face value, copyright means (as the Copyright Office in Washington, DC, aptly explains) "the right to copy." In other words, when you create an original work (such as a song), you own exclusive rights to that work. The reason you acquired those rights is because the U.S. Copyright Act exists.

Publication, on the other hand, is defined by the copyright law as "the distribution of copies or phonorecords [see p. nineteen for a definition of phonorecords] of a work to the public by sale or other transfer of ownership, or by rental, lease, or lending." A published work can also be a work for which there has been an "offering to distribute copies or phonorecords to a group of persons for purposes of further distribution, public performance, or public display."

What the copyright law is saying is that publication doesn't necessarily take effect even when copies are actually printed or pressed. There must also be distribution of copies or an "offering to distribute copies" before something is considered to be published.

I realize these aren't indepth definitions of the terms "copyright" and "publication," but both concepts will receive a lot of coverage in the pages ahead, beginning with some background information on copyright.

Publication doesn't necessarily take effect even when copies are actually printed or pressed. There must also be distribution of copies or an "offering to distribute copies."

A LITTLE COPYRIGHT HISTORY

The concept of the copyright is based, primarily, on logic and law. If you create something original, you should be protected from unauthorized copying of your original work. Long before there were copyright laws there was a commandment that made the same point: "Thou shalt not steal."

But along with protection from theft, copyright laws were also devised as an inducement for a country's citizens to *create* copyrightable works. If there was no protection and compensation (or the possibility of compensation) for writing songs, books or plays, or for creating other types of copyrightable material, creative people would be forced to earn their livings in other ways. Of course, many would continue to create original works in any event, but it is unquestionable that the volume of creative works would be greatly reduced without the incentive which copyright laws provide.

In the United States before 1788, Congress didn't have the power to constitute a federal copyright act. When Noah Webster wanted to prevent others from copying his latest work, *American Spelling Book*, he campaigned for copyright legislation in this country.

In response to his efforts, on May 2, 1783, Congress made a recommendation to the thirteen states that they should each create legislation that would protect authors and publishers of books. (As you can see, even at the beginning of copyright history in this country, copyrights and publishing were linked together.) By 1787, twelve of the states had copyright laws in place. All twelve states had used a British law dating from 1710—the Statute of Queen Anne—as their basic guide.

In 1788 the Constitution was ratified, giving Congress the power, in the Constitution's words, "To promote the Progress of Science and useful Arts, by securing for limited Times to Authors and Inventors the exclusive Right to their respective Writings and Discoveries."

Congress quickly went to work and created the U.S. Copyright Act of 1790, once again patterning the law after the Statute of Queen Anne—a statute that was extremely limited and filled with restrictions and registration requirements.

The first federal copyright law gave protection to books, charts and maps created by U.S. citizens and residents.

This first federal copyright law gave protection to books, charts and maps created by U.S. citizens and residents. Apparently, popular songs (and other types of music) were not yet considered "useful Arts" by Congress.

(Luckily for songwriters, Congress finally added musical compositions to the copyright law in 1831. Before this new provision, some early music publishers had already begun putting musical selections together and selling them as a book—thus receiving copyright protection under the 1790 law.)

To be guaranteed copyright protection under the 1790 law, one had to record the title, before it was published, at the clerk's office of the local district court; have a copy of this fact printed in at least one newspaper for four weeks; and send a copy of the actual book, chart or map to the Secretary of State's office any time during the first six months after it had been published.

Since the Constitution said that the law should be in effect "for limited Times," the 1790 copyright law said an author's work would be protected for fourteen years, with the right to one renewal term of an additional fourteen years.

The purpose of putting a limit on the duration of a copyright is to preclude the failure "to promote the Progress of . . . useful Arts." The idea behind this portion of Article I of the Constitution was to prevent a permanent monopoly on a copyright. Thus, under the 1790 law, once the original term of copyright neared expiration, it was necessary to renew the copyright by going through the business with the clerk's office and the newspaper again.

If these steps for proper renewal weren't taken, the once-copyrighted work fell into the public domain. Once in the public domain, the book, chart or map became public property and could be reprinted without anyone having to account to the former copyright owner. Needless to say, allowing a copyright to go "PD" before the end of its full twenty-eight year life span was the ultimate faux pas among copyright owners.

The purpose of putting a limit on the duration of a copyright is to prevent a permanent monopoly on a copyright.

Even if properly renewed, twenty-eight years was as long as a copyright could last at that time. If a book's copyright went into effect in 1800, the book went PD by 1829 no matter what. If the author was twenty years old in the initial copyright year, he lost all rights to his own creation by the time he was forty-nine.

Included in a number of new rules added in 1831 was the extension of the first term of copyright to twenty-eight years, with the renewal term remaining at fourteen. Now a songwriter's work had the potential to be protected for a total of forty-two years.

The loss of a copyright during the copyright creator's lifetime has been a major problem throughout the history of U.S. copyright law. If you began writing songs after December 31, 1977, it is a problem you're not likely to face. However, thousands of copyright owners whose works were in the first term of copyright prior to 1978 fall into a unique category that will require more detailed explanation. [See "Length of Copyright Protection," p. 27.]

In 1897 Congress added the concept of public performance rights. Although several more years would pass before all of the wrinkles were ironed out, the copyright owner now had the right to be paid for public performances of the copyrighted work. The payment of royalties for the public performance of a copyrighted musical work would later become one of the most important sources of income for composers, lyricists and music publishers.

The Copyright Act of 1909 was a major overhaul of the previous copyright statutes. In one big, all-encompassing act, all of the provisions for copyright protection were laid out. One new provision was that the period for the copyright renewal term was now twenty-eight years, making the potential life of a song fifty-six years before entering the public domain.

As I mentioned in chapter one, the 1909 act required that a two-cent royalty be paid on copyrighted songs that were reproduced mechanically. At that time, the law was referring to piano rolls and early disc and cylinder recordings. As technology progressed, the law later applied to other forms of mechanical reproduction such as electrical transcriptions and audio tapes.

By 1955, technology and new art forms were making the 1909 act seem quite antiquated, so the Copyright Office—with funding from Congress—began studies in preparation for a major revision of the 1909 law. While these studies were still ongoing, Congress decided to extend the life of many copyrights that would have begun entering the public domain in the latter part of 1962.

Working out the many details of a copyright act suitable for the second half of the twentieth century proved to be a difficult task. There were factions whose livelihoods might be improved by a new copyright law, while other factions might have to pay out higher royalties or royalties not previously required. After extensive lobbying on all sides, the new copyright law was enacted on October 19, 1976, essentially becoming effective on January 1, 1978.

This new copyright law changed the duration of a copyright, in most cases, to the life of the author plus fifty years for works created after December 31, 1977. There were several other substantial changes from the 1909 law, many of which are still in effect today.

Why aren't *all* of the changes still in effect today? One reason is because of something called the Berne Convention Implementation Act of 1988, which allowed the United States to become part of the world's most significant international copyright treaty. Former president Ronald Reagan signed the Berne Act on October 31, 1988, with the law becoming effective on March 1, 1989. The Berne Act changed only some portions of the 1976 Copyright Act, much of which remains intact [See "Highlights of U.S. Adherence to the Berne Convention," pp. 20-21].

Ironically, there have been changes in copyright law since the implementation of the Berne Act in 1989, so some of the "Highlights" listed (such as the heading "Renewal is Still Required") are no longer accurate (as you will see in the section on p. 27, "Length of Copyright Protection"). One of the things to keep in mind is that copyright law is not static. To quote Martha Stewart, "It's a good thing." Otherwise, we might all still be living under the Statute of Queen Anne.

COPYRIGHT—SOME GENERAL THOUGHTS

Now that you're familiar with some areas of copyright law from a historical standpoint, it's time to get into the specifics of the law currently in effect. Two of the topics most songwriters seem to be concerned about are registration of copyrights and copyright infringement. Both subjects are important and both will be covered in this book, but of equal importance is a general knowledge of what copyright protection is and what it means to you as a copyright owner.

If you haven't already learned about copyright law from a reliable source, you might discover a few surprises here. For instance, you may have heard that you have to fill out a form and send it to the Copyright Office for your song to be "copyrighted." Or, you might have been told that it's okay to copy a specific number of measures from another song without being guilty of copyright infringement. These are just a couple of copyright law myths that we'll dispose of in the following pages.

One of the main things you're about to discover is that there are several terms and phrases used in discussions about copyright with which you might not already be familiar. Just as in learning a foreign language, there are lots of words in the music publishing business that must become a part of your vocabulary.

Just as in learning a foreign language, there are lots of words in the music publishing business that must become a part of your vocabulary.

I learned to speak "music business" over the course of many years and am now at a point where I can hold my own in a roomful of record company executives, musicians, entertainment lawyers and accountants. Recently, though, I finally stepped into the world of the Internet. Before I began to learn the terminology, I didn't know what my web-obsessed friends were talking about. Once I entered cyberspace myself, I was forced to learn "cyberspeak." Soon I could converse with my friends on their level.

The point is, to be able to communicate knowledgeably with music publishers and entertainment lawyers you need to be able to speak and understand their language. Once you learn the terminology, you may find yourself more fluent than a lot of people already in the music publishing business—a very enviable position for any songwriter.

FIVE EXCLUSIVE RIGHTS OF THE COPYRIGHT OWNER

With several notable limitations, the U.S. Copyright Act gives the copyright owner "the exclusive right to do and to authorize others to do" five specific activities:

1. [The right] "to reproduce the copyrighted work in copies or phonorecords."

    Here we come across the word "phonorecords" again. The definition provided by the 1976 Copyright Act says that phonorecords are:

    > material objects in which sounds, other than those accompanying a motion picture or other audiovisual work, are fixed by any method now known or later developed, and from which the sounds can be perceived, reproduced, or otherwise communicated, either directly or with the aid of a machine or device. The term "phonorecords" includes the material object in which the sounds are first fixed.

    A phonorecord, then, can be a prerecorded audiotape, a record of any speed (remember those?), a compact disc, or any other device that falls into the category of the definition, whether "now known or later developed." When this definition was devised, commercial sales of compact discs didn't exist. Luckily for copyright owners, the definition of phonorecords in the 1976 Copyright Act provided for such future inventions so that revisions in the law wouldn't be required with each new technological development.

    Now that we know what phonorecords are, let's get back to the first exclusive right listed above: a copyright owner has the right to (or authorize others to) "reproduce the copyrighted work in copies or phonorecords."

    Once you have written a song, you have the exclusive right to reproduce copies of that song. If you want to print sheet music of your song, the law says that's one of your rights. Conversely, if someone else wants to reproduce copies of your song, they can do so only if you authorize them to, or if they fall into the category of those exempt from this provision of the copyright law.

    Once you have written a song, you have the exclusive right to reproduce copies of that song.

    So who's exempt, and why? Earlier, when I said the copyright law gives you some exclusive rights, I prefaced the sentence with the phrase "with several notable limitations." Sometimes copyright law seems a lot like English grammar. For every rule there seems to be at least one exception. Rather than dwell on the exceptions now, I'll discuss all of them together later in the section on "Limitations of Exclusive Rights."

    Allowing the *initial* reproduction of your copyrighted work on phonorecords is an exclusive right that has no limitations. However, once that initial recording has been distributed, anyone can record your copyrighted work as long as a notice of intention is given to you and proper royalties are paid. As you will recall, the 1909 Copyright Act called for a mechanical royalty of two cents per unit. This provision was updated in the 1976 law and will be discussed in detail later under the heading "The Compulsory Mechanical License."

    Allowing the initial *reproduction of your copyrighted work on phonorecords is an exclusive right that has no limitations.*

2. [The right] "to prepare derivative works based upon the copyrighted work."

    Here we are again with another term that doesn't come up in everyday conversation. According to the 1976 Copyright Act definition, a derivative work is:

Highlights of
U.S. Adherence to the Berne Convention

On March 1, 1989, the United States joined the Berne Union by entering into an international treaty called the Berne Convention, whose full title is the Berne Convention for the Protection of Literary and Artistic Works. Also on March 1, 1989, amendments to the U.S. copyright law that satisfy U.S. treaty obligations under the Convention took effect. The U.S. law continues to govern the protection and registration of works in the United States. The following discussion outlines the most important amendments in the law.

EFFECT OF U.S. MEMBERSHIP IN THE BERNE UNION

Beginning March 1, 1989, copyright in the works of U.S. authors will be protected automatically in all member nations of the Berne Union. (As of September 1988, there were a total of 79 member nations in the Berne Union.)

Since members of the Berne Union agree to a certain minimum level of copyright protection, each Berne Union country will provide at least that guaranteed level for U.S. authors.

Members of the Berne Union agree to treat nationals of other member countries like their own nationals for purposes of copyright. Therefore, U.S. authors will often receive higher levels of protection than the guaranteed minimum.

Overall, piracy of U.S. works abroad can be fought more effectively.

Beginning March 1, 1989, works of foreign authors who are nationals of a Berne Union country and works first published in a Berne Union country are automatically protected in the United States.

U.S. LAW AMENDED

In order to fulfill its Berne Convention obligations, the United States made certain changes in its copyright law by passing the Berne Convention Implementation Act of 1988. These changes are not retroactive and are effective only on and after March 1, 1989.

Mandatory Notice of Copyright Is Abolished

Mandatory notice of copyright has been abolished for works published for the first time on or after March 1, 1989. Failure to place a notice of copyright on copies or phonorecords of such works can no longer result in the loss of copyright.

Voluntary use of notice is encouraged. Placing a notice of copyright on published works is still strongly recommended. One of the benefits is that an infringer will not be able to claim that he or she "innocently infringed" a work. (A successful innocent infringement claim may result in a reduction in damages for infringement that the copyright owner would otherwise receive.)

A sample notice of copyright is: © 1989 John Brown.

The notice requirement for works incorporating a predominant portion of U.S. government work has been eliminated as of March 1, 1989. For these works to receive the evidentiary benefit of voluntary notice, in addition to the notice, a statement is required on the copies identifying what is copyrighted.

A sample is: © 1989 Jane Brown. Copyright claimed in Chapters 7-10, exclusive of U.S. government maps.

Notice Unchanged for Works Published Before March 1, 1989

The Berne Convention Implementation Act is not retroactive. Thus, the notice requirements that were in place before March 1, 1989, govern all works first published during that period (regardless of national origin).

- Works first published between January 1, 1978, and February 28, 1989: If a work was first published without notice during this period, it is still necessary to register the work before or within five years after publication and add the notice to copies distributed in the United States after discovery of the omission.
- Works first published before January 1, 1978: If a work was first published without the required notice before 1978, copyright was lost immediately (except for works seeking "ad interim" protection). Once copyright is lost, it can never be restored in the United States, except by special legislation.

Mandatory Deposit

Copyright owners must deposit in the Copyright Office two complete copies or phonorecords of the best edition of all works subject to copyright that are publicly distributed in the United States, whether or not the work contains a notice of copyright. In general, this deposit requirement may be satisfied by registration. For more information about mandatory deposit, request Circular 7d.

Registration as a Prerequisite to Suit

Before a copyright infringement suit is brought for a work of U.S. origin, it must be submitted to the Copyright Office for registration.

When is the United States the country of origin of a work? The United States is the country of origin if:

- Publication first occurred in the United States.
- Publication occurred simultaneously in the United States and a non-Berne Union country. "Simultaneous publication" means within the first 30 days of publication.
- Publication occurred simultaneously in the United States and another Berne Union country that provides the same term as or a longer term of protection than the United States.
- The work is unpublished and all of the authors are nationals of the United States. (U.S. domiciliaries and habitual residents are treated the same as nationals.) In the case of an unpublished audiovisual work, all the authors are legal entities with headquarters in the United States.
- The work is a pictorial, graphic, or sculptural work that is incorporated in a permanent structure located in the United States.
- The work is first published in a non-Berne Union country and all of the authors are U.S. nationals. In the case of a published audiovisual work, all the authors are legal entities with headquarters in the United States.

Although Berne Convention works whose origin is **not** the United States are exempt from the requirement to register before suit can be brought, a person seeking the exemption bears the burden of proving to the court that the work is not subject to the registration requirement.

Benefits of Registration

Berne Convention works whose country of origin is not the United States need not be registered with the Copyright Office in order to bring an infringement suit. However, registration is still strongly recommended.

Presumption of copyright validity. The copyright owner who registers before or within five years of first publication receives the benefit of a legal presumption in court, called prima facie evidentiary weight. This means that the court will presume:

- that the facts stated in the copyright certificate of registration are true; and
- that the copyright is valid.

Statutory damages and attorney's fees. Another benefit of timely registration is that the copyright owner of works registered for copyright protection within three months of publication, or before infringement, is eligible for an award of attorney's fees and statutory damages. These damages are now double the amounts previously provided. A copyright owner may elect to receive either actual damages or statutory damages. Where statutory damages are elected, the court determines the amount of the award, within a certain range. The Berne Convention Implementation Act doubles statutory damages to:

- A range between $500 and $20,000 for ordinary infringement;
- A maximum of $100,000 for willful infringement; and
- A minimum of $200 for innocent infringement.

Renewal Is Still Required

Works first federally copyrighted before 1978 must still be renewed in the 28th year in order to receive the second term of 47 years. If such a work is not timely renewed, it will fall into the public domain in the United States at the end of the 28th year.

Recordation

Recordation as a Prerequisite to an Infringement Suit. The copyright owner no longer has to record a transfer before bringing a copyright lawsuit in that owner's name.

Benefits of recordation. The benefits of recordation in the Copyright Office are unchanged:

- Under certain conditions, recordation establishes priorities between conflicting transfers and nonexclusive licenses;
- Under certain conditions, recordation establishes priority between conflicting transfers; and,
- Recordation establishes a public record of the contents of the transfer or document.

Jukebox Licenses

Section 116 of the 1976 Copyright Act provides for a compulsory license to publicly perform nondramatic musical works by means of coin-operated phonorecord players (jukeboxes). The Berne Convention Implementation Act amends the law to provide for negotiated licenses between the user (the jukebox operator) and the copyright owner. If necessary, the parties are encouraged to submit to arbitration to facilitate negotiated licenses. Such licenses take precedence over the compulsory license.

a work based upon one or more pre-existing works, such as a translation, music arrangement, dramatization, fictionalization, motion picture version, sound recording, art reproduction, abridgement, condensation, or any other form in which a work may be recast, transformed, or adapted. A work consisting of editorial revisions, annotations, elaborations or other modifications which, as a whole, represent an original work of authorship, is a "derivative work."

A derivative work, then, can be a number of different things. One example would be the addition of lyrics to an instrumental work that has already gone into the public domain. For instance, if you added lyrics to Beethoven's Fifth Symphony, the result would be copyrightable by you under the definition of "derivative work." Of course, since Beethoven's compositions are in the public domain, anyone else who wished to could also add their own lyrics to that melody without requiring your permission. Theirs would simply be another derivative work derived from the same music. The fact that your derivative work is copyrightable doesn't mean that Beethoven's Fifth Symphony suddenly wouldn't be in the public domain anymore. Only the derivative work that you created (the combination of your lyrics and his music) would be copyrightable.

To change the situation slightly, let's say you have created an original instrumental piece. To make things more interesting, let's say that it became a big hit due to its use in a popular movie. If you allow someone to add lyrics to your instrumental hit, the result would be a derivative work that would be copyrightable. Of course, in this situation, you would have to come to an agreement with the lyricist as to how royalties would be shared in this new derivative work since your original copyright is still alive and well.

On the other hand, if someone adds lyrics to your instrumental piece without your permission, the result is an unauthorized derivative work—an infringement of your copyright. Why? Because the law says you, the copyright owner, have the exclusive right to prepare, or authorize others to prepare, a derivative work. If someone has created an unauthorized derivative work of your copyright, you have the right to enter into that time-honored music industry tradition of suing the unauthorized party.

The law says you, the copyright owner, have the exclusive right to prepare, or authorize others to prepare, a derivative work.

One type of derivative work which is very prevalent today occurs when a recording artist takes a preexisting recording of a song and "samples" it to such an extent that the new work created by the sampler is merely a derivative work of the original. (For a thorough explanation of "sampling," see p. 53.) For example, let's say I wrote and recorded a song called "Mary Had a Miniature Infant Sheep." Then let's say that another recording artist sampled a large section of my song, added a rap lyric to it, and left my original chorus in. In fact, his version is so derivative of my song, he even wants to call his song "Mary Had a Miniature Infant Sheep, Uh-Huh!" Assuming I am willing to allow the new lyrics to be added, his recording of "Mary Had a Miniature Infant Sheep, Uh-Huh!" would be a derivative work of my song. As I am the copyright owner of the original work, whether he would be allowed to share in the writing credits or the publishing income would be my decision.

3. [The right] "to distribute copies or phonorecords of the copyrighted work to the public by sale or other transfer of ownership, or by rental, lease, or lending."

   You already know that the first exclusive right listed gives you the right to reproduce copies of your copyrighted work. Here the law goes on to say that another of your rights is to (or authorize others to) distribute those copies (such as sheet music) for sale to the public. As I mentioned in chapter one, today there are print publishers who specialize in the printing, distribution and selling of sheet music, folios and other printed versions of a musical composition. However, they can only do so if they have been authorized to by the owner of the copyrighted work.

   Regarding the distribution of phonorecords, the same rule applies except that, as I mentioned earlier, after the initial recording has been made, others may distribute new recordings of the song as long as a notice of intention has been given to the copyright owner and as long as the royalties required by law are properly paid.

   If you refer to the definition of publication at the beginning of this chapter, you will see that this third exclusive right is actually your right to publish your work (or to authorize others to publish it).

4. [The right] "to perform the copyrighted work publicly, in the case of literary, musical, dramatic, and choreographic works, pantomimes, and motion pictures and other audiovisual works."

   The performance right is one of the most valuable rights a songwriter has. In its most basic form, this means that (with the exceptions granted by copyright law) no one has the right to perform your song in public except you or those you authorize.

   Of course, once you've written a song, it is likely that you're going to want it to be performed in public as often as possible. Also, although it is possible to stop the unlawful copying or distribution of your song, it would be a pretty difficult task to keep track of all the singers who might be performing your work at any given moment.

   As a result of the fact that public performance is one of the rights of the copyright holder, there are now three performing rights societies in the United States: ASCAP, BMI and SESAC. Their function is to charge licensing fees to a variety of sources which use publicly performed music, including radio stations, television stations, concert halls and nightclubs. Most of the money received by the performing rights societies is then paid to songwriters and publishers. How much money is due to which songwriter and publisher is determined by the various monitoring systems and payment plans that have been devised by each of the performing rights societies. All three societies will be covered in detail in chapter four.

   Three performing rights societies charge licensing fees to a variety of sources which use publicly performed music, including radio stations, television stations, concert halls and nightclubs.

5. [The right] "to display the copyrighted work publicly, in the case of literary, musical, dramatic, and choreographic works, pantomimes, and pictorial, graphic, or sculptural works, including the individual images of a motion picture or other audiovisual work."

   Of the five exclusive rights of the copyright owner, the "right to display" probably ranks as the least important for songwriters and music publishers. Unlike well-behaved children, songs are usually heard but not seen. Therefore, it's relatively rare that a song would fall into the category of being displayable.

However, when a song appears in sheet music form, the "displayability" becomes apparent. If the sponsor of a print advertisement wishes to use a piece of sheet music as a part of his ad, permission to do so would have to be requested of the copyright owner.

Occasionally a book about popular music may display a piece of sheet music on the book's cover or as part of the text. This type of use would also require permission from the copyright owner.

And, in the case of Karaoke, the words to a popular song are displayed on a video screen while a prerecorded instrumental track is being played. For the lyrics to be displayed, permission of the copyright owner is required under this portion of the copyright law.

As you can surmise, the exclusive right to display would be of extreme importance to the copyright owners of photographs, artwork, motion pictures, and other copyrightable materials that more readily lend themselves to exhibition.

LIMITATIONS OF EXCLUSIVE RIGHTS

The Law giveth and the Law taketh away. As soon as the Copyright Act finishes outlining the copyright owner's five exclusive rights, it then takes several pages to explain all of the limitations of those rights.

The first limitation covered in the act is a concept called "fair use." The fair use exception applies to all five exclusive rights "for purposes such as criticism, comment, news reporting, teaching (including multiple copies for classroom use), scholarship, or research. . . ."

Provided that the use of a copyrighted work falls into the fair use category, that particular use is not considered to be an infringement of the copyright.

Provided that the use of a copyrighted work falls into the fair use category, that particular use is not considered to be an infringement of the copyright.

The Copyright Act goes on to say that there are four factors to consider in determining what is a fair use. These are:

1. the purpose and character of the use, including whether such use is of a commercial nature or is for nonprofit educational purposes;

2. the nature of the copyrighted work;

3. the amount and substantiality of the portion used in relation to the copyrighted work as a whole; and

4. the effect of the use upon the potential market for or value of the copyrighted work.

Since it would be impossible to cover every conceivable variation of what a fair use might be, the law is saying that these are the four guidelines that would be considered if a copyright owner should question whether or not a particular use of the owner's work is a fair use.

Under the fair use guidelines provided by the Copyright Act, there are clearly exceptions to the copyright owner's exclusive right "to reproduce the copyrighted work in copies."

Regarding the owner's exclusive right "to reproduce the copyrighted work in . . . phonorecords," the limitations include the right of libraries and archives to make phonorecords in specific situations. Music educators may also make recordings of student performances for study and for school archives.

The other major limitation on the owner's exclusive right to reproduce phonorecords falls in the category of compulsory mechanical licenses. [See "The Compulsory Mechanical License," below.]

Limitations regarding the right to "prepare derivative works based upon the copyrighted work" are not specifically covered by the Copyright Act except in its brief section on fair use, in which case all five exclusive rights are limited. However, it is generally agreed that printed copies that have been purchased can be edited or simplified for educational purposes as long as the fundamental character of the work isn't distorted or the lyrics changed.

In reference to the exclusive right "to *distribute* copies or phonorecords of the copyrighted work to the public by sale . . . ," there is no limitation except that provided under fair use and by the compulsory license requirement regarding recordings of a song after the initial recording has been released.

The Copyright Act lists several specific limitations on the right to perform or display copyrighted works publicly. Among these are:

1. Performance or display of a work by instructors or pupils in the course of face-to-face teaching activities of a nonprofit educational institution;

2. Performance or display of a work on closed circuit TV to other classrooms or to disabled students for teaching purposes if the transmission is part of the systematic instructional activities of a nonprofit educational institution;

3. Performance of a work at a concert if there is no purpose of direct or indirect commercial advantage, no fee or compensation paid to the performers, promoters, or organizers, and no admission charge. If there is an admission charge, all of the proceeds must be used for educational, religious, or charitable purposes; and

4. Performance of works of a religious nature in the course of services at places of worship or at a religious assembly.

The Copyright Act goes on to list limitations on exclusive rights as they pertain to ephemeral recordings, secondary transmissions, reproductions of pictorial, graphic, and sculptural works and on and on. Rather than get bogged down in seemingly endless limitations, let's move on to an area that is of utmost importance to both songwriters and music publishers.

THE COMPULSORY MECHANICAL LICENSE

The compulsory mechanical license allows recording companies (or anyone else who wishes) the right to record and release a copyrighted composition without obtaining permission from the copyright owner as long as: 1) an initial release of a phonorecord of the song has already taken place in the United States with the copyright owner's permission, and 2) those subsequently recording and releasing the song on phonorecords adhere to the compulsory mechanical license rules as described in the copyright law.

Compulsory licenses became a part of the Copyright Act in 1909. The 1909 act said that someone wishing to record and distribute a published musical work via a mechanical device (in those days the law was referring to piano rolls, cylinder recordings and early disc recordings) could do so provided that a notice of intention was given and the proper fees were paid to the copyright owner.

Under the 1976 law, "Any person who wishes to obtain a compulsory license . . . shall, before or within thirty days after making, and before distributing any phonorecords of the work, serve notice of intention to do so on the copyright owner. If the registration or other public record of the Copyright Office do not identify the copyright owner and include an address at which notice can be served, it shall be sufficient to file the notice of intention in the Copyright Office." The licensee is also required to make monthly payments to the copyright owner, with an accounting statement rendered "under oath" detailing the number of phonorecords distributed during the previous month.

The 1976 law also outlines other types of compulsory licenses for noncommercial educational broadcasting and for secondary transmissions by cable systems. However, the compulsory license that has the most important ramifications for songwriters and publishers is the compulsory mechanical license.

This concept was originally created to prevent a monopoly by the Aeolian Co., a company that had entered into lengthy contracts with the major music publishers around the turn of the twentieth century. The Aeolian Co. manufactured piano rolls and had caused other companies to be cut out of the lucrative business of making piano rolls of the most popular songs of the day because those titles were all exclusively signed to Aeolian.

The compulsory mechanical license that was created by the 1909 Copyright Act gave the other piano roll companies a loophole of sorts by which they could have access to the same popular songs as Aeolian. This concept would later prevent any one record company from having an exclusive license on any particular song.

Consider for a moment what the situation might be today if the compulsory mechanical license had never been created. If the Beatles' American record label had all of their songs signed to exclusive contracts, a song like "Yesterday" could be recorded only by artists on that particular label. Because of the compulsory mechanical license, hundreds of artists on hundreds of different record labels have recorded "Yesterday," turning it into one of the most popular songs of all time.

There have also been many cases where songs originally recorded on small labels later became hits because they were released on a major label. For songwriters and music publishers the importance of the compulsory mechanical license concept can't be overstated.

Despite that importance, however, the procedures involved in the proper implementation of the compulsory license (the notice of intention, monthly accountings, etc.) make it quite cumbersome. The many rules involved in properly adhering to the requirements of the compulsory license have resulted in a concept known as the "negotiated mechanical license." This negotiated license is used in the music

The "negotiated mechanical license" is used to bypass the complexities of the compulsory mechanical license while still adhering to the copyright law. Its use has resulted in a major source of music publishing income in modern times.

industry today to bypass the complexities of the compulsory mechanical license while still adhering to the copyright law.

The negotiated mechanical license isn't a part of the copyright law, but I mention it now because its use has resulted in a major source of music publishing income in modern times. Negotiated mechanical licenses and mechanical royalties will be discussed in detail at the beginning of chapter four.

THE COPYRIGHT OWNER

A copyright exists by virtue of the fact that it has been created by the process of authorship. The Copyright Act says that ownership of a copyright "vests initially in the author or authors of the work." What all of this means is that the person who writes the song is the initial copyright owner.

The law goes on to say that "the authors of a joint work are co-owners of copyright in the work." In other words, unless the writers have an agreement to the contrary, each writer who contributes to the creation of a particular song is a co-owner of that song.

Are there exceptions to these rules? As you have probably surmised by now, exceptions exist throughout the copyright law. In the case of copyright ownership, there is one particularly problematic exception to the general rule that the true author of a work is the initial copyright claimant. The exception in this case is something called a "work made for hire." A "work made for hire" is defined in the law as "a work prepared by an employee within the scope of his or her employment" or "a work specially ordered or commissioned" for use in one of nine different categories,* if the parties agree in writing that the work is to be for hire, even if the creator is not an employee in the traditional sense.

A while back I wrote liner notes for a particular record company. Under our agreement, everything I wrote for the company was a "work made for hire." Although I was the creator of the work, my employer was the author of the work under the Copyright Act.

As a songwriter, you should generally avoid contracts that describe your song as a "work made for hire." However, there are certain times when such a situation is almost unavoidable. Unless you are practically a superstar, writing a film or TV score or a commercial jingle will usually require your doing so as a "work made for hire." Also, staff songwriter deals are sometimes made "for hire."

In some cases, at least in the early stages of your career, a "work made for hire" clause is just a part of life. As you will see in chapter six, though, most other times a "work made for hire" situation should be avoided.

LENGTH OF COPYRIGHT PROTECTION

As you have already learned, the length of time that a copyright is protected has changed dramatically over the years. As this book is going to press, the current length to copyright protection is from the moment a song is created until fifty years after the songwriter dies. There is a major move afoot to extend the length of a

---

*For the curious, the nine categories are: (1) as a contribution to a collective work; (2) as a part of a motion picture or other audiovisual work; (3) as a translation; (4) as a supplementary work; (5) as a compilation; (6) as an instructional text; (7) as a test; (8) as answer material for a test; or (9) as an atlas.

copyright in the U.S. to "life of the author plus seventy years," as is already the case in many other countries.

Therefore, if you are a relatively new songwriter, the length of copyright protection for your songs—under normal circumstances—is from the moment they are created until (most likely) seventy years after your unfortunate passing. The key phrases here are "relatively new songwriter" and "under normal circumstances." The truth is that there are actually a variety of lengths of copyright protection currently in effect.

Earlier I said that the 1976 Copyright Act changed the duration of a copyright for works created after December 31, 1977. But what happened to those songs written prior to 1978? Before I attempt to answer that, let's have a quick review of copyright law in effect prior to 1978.

Under the 1909 Copyright Act, a copyright lasted for twenty-eight years. During the twenty-eighth year, a renewal had to be filed with the Copyright Office for the copyright to be extended for another twenty-eight years, making the total length of that copyright fifty-six years.

So what happened to all of those pre-1978 songs when the new law went into effect? The renewal term was extended from twenty-eight years to forty-seven years, making the total possible length of a copyright for a pre-1978 song seventy-five years.

If a copyright was already in renewal, the renewal term was automatically extended to forty-seven years. But, the 1976 Copyright Act still called for those songs originally copyrighted between January 1, 1950 and December 31, 1977 to have renewal forms filed with the Copyright Office during the twenty-eighth year of copyright for the forty-seven year renewal term to take effect. Otherwise, the copyright would expire at the end of the first twenty-eight years.

In other words, despite the fact that songs being written today have a copyright span of "life-plus-fifty" (no doubt, soon to be "life-plus-seventy"), there are thousands of pre-1978 songs that still had to be renewed when those copyrights reached their twenty-eighth year to receive the additional forty-seven years of copyright protection.

For example, the song "Jailhouse Rock" was written by Jerry Leiber and Mike Stoller in 1957. In 1985, the twenty-eighth year of the copyright, a Form RE was filed with the Copyright Office, giving the song an additional forty-seven years of copyright protection.

Then, on June 26, 1992, Public Law 102-307 was enacted, amending the copyright law to automatically extend the term of copyrights secured between January 1, 1964 and December 31, 1977 to a further term of forty-seven years. This made the filing of the RE form optional for those works. The huge advantage to this new law is that copyright owners whose songs were originally copyrighted between 1964 and 1977 no longer have to wory about their songs going into the public domain due to failure to file the proper form.

But, if you wrote your first song on or after January 1, 1978, your copyrights will still be in effect until (assuming the law changes) seventy years after you've gone to Rock & Roll Heaven, right? In almost all cases, the answer is "yes." The exceptions are works made for hire and anonymous or pseudonymous works, in which case the length of copyright is either seventy-five years from first publication or one hundred years from creation, whichever is shorter. Already you can probably see one of the problems inherent in a work made for hire. Although you may not live to see a work made for hire expire after seventy-five years, your heirs may not be able to enjoy the financial benefits of your work nearly as long as they would if your creation hadn't been made for hire.

If your copyright is not a work made for hire, and if you write under an assumed name or anonymously, the copyright duration will still be "life-plus-fifty" (or seventy) if you reveal your real name when you register your songs with the Copyright Office. [See the sample registration form, pp. 39-40.]

If you are concerned about your heirs, you might be interested to know that when a song is written by two or more people, the copyright continues to exist for fifty (or seventy) years "after the last surviving author's death." This rule has prompted a few songwriters I know to list their children as co-writers on songs written after 1977. Whether this practice is strictly legal may be questionable. We won't know for sure unless it is eventually challenged by someone in a court of law.

THE COPYRIGHT NOTICE

There was a time in the not-too-distant past when failure to place a copyright notice on visually perceptible copies of a song meant losing the copyright entirely. Beginning with the original U.S. Copyright Act of 1790, the copyright notice has been an important part of the law.

Until the 1976 copyright law was enacted, omitting the copyright notice or putting it in the wrong place on a piece of sheet music could result in the song going into the public domain.

Luckily, the 1976 law was much more reasonable, allowing the failure to include the copyright notice, or some technical error regarding the notice, to be correctable. If you followed the Copyright Act's "procedures for correcting errors and omissions of the copyright notice on works published on or after January 1, 1978," your copyright would not be lost.

The good news today is that the current copyright statute (as amended to comply with the Berne Convention) says that failure to properly affix the copyright notice on a work created on or after March 1, 1989, cannot cause that work to enter the public domain.

Failure to properly affix the copyright notice on a work created on or after March 1, 1989, cannot cause that work to enter the public domain.

So what is this copyright notice and what makes it so important? First of all, if you own sheet music, records, posters or anything else that is copyrightable, you've seen copyright notices before. It is that familiar little "c" with a circle around it, followed by a particular year and the name of the copyright owner. If you look near the front of this book you will see a notice that says (© 1997 by Randy Poe).

Here are the exact specifications that the Copyright Office requires for a technically correct copyright notice should you choose to include one:

1. The symbol © or the word "Copyright" or the abbreviation "Copr.," followed by
2. The year of the first publication of the work, followed by
3. The name of the copyright owner of the work in question.

This notice has to appear on one of the first pages of copies of published works that are visually perceptible. The purpose of this notice is to let the public know that a work is protected by copyright, the year of first publication, and who the copyright owner is. If a copyright notice appears on a visually perceptible copy of a work, the public is being put on notice that this published work can't be copied without permission of the copyright owner (although lack of a notice doesn't mean copying *is* allowed). One would be taking a chance to copy a piece of music just because it doesn't have a copyright notice.

If the current law says you don't have to worry about your song going PD if you leave the copyright notice off, then what's the big deal? The answer is that someone acquiring a copy of your published song with no copyright notice on it might assume that the song is in the public domain. If that person uses your work and can prove that he or she was misled by the fact that there was no notice, you could suffer a loss of certain damages that might otherwise have been recovered from that party in an infringement suit.

We've already briefly covered the concept of "publication." The year of publication is the year that is listed on the copyright notice. In the matter of unpublished works, the Copyright Office suggests for your own protection that you place the words "Unpublished Work" prior to your copyright notice. For example, if I were to write a song in 1999, at the bottom of my lead sheet I could write "Unpublished Work Copyright 1999 Randy Poe."

AREAS NOT PROTECTED BY COPYRIGHT

Songs that are "original works of authorship" and that have been "fixed in a tangible form of expression" are protected under federal copyright law. So why should songwriters care about what's not protected?

Well, there are actually a couple of noncopyrightable areas that pertain to songwriters. Perhaps the most important of these is the *title*. If you write a song called "I Love My Dog," someone else can write another song with the same title. Obviously the lyrics and music will have to be different from yours (with the possible exception of the phrase "I love my dog"), but the fact remains that your song title isn't protected by copyright law.

Your song title isn't protected by copyright law.

Does this mean you're free to sit down and write a song called "Rudolph the Red-Nosed Reindeer"? Not really. In the case of a title that has reached the point of having a secondary meaning, laws regarding unfair competition can be put to use.

Unfair competition laws generally prevent someone from attempting to confuse the public by making them think that another's property is his; in other words, by "passing off" a more notable creation as his own. Since most people would consider "Rudolph the Red-Nosed Reindeer" to be the title of one particular song of a certain melody and specific lyrics, the title has become so closely identified with the Johnny Marks composition that it means *only* that song and no other. So, the public would expect any released recording of a song entitled "Rudolph the Red-Nosed Reindeer" to be the one by Johnny Marks. The title has thus acquired a secondary meaning—Johnny Marks's song about one of Santa's reindeer—to the extent that others can be prevented from using it as their title for a different song.

If you keep in mind that one of the major points of writing a song is to create

something new and original, you shouldn't have a problem coming up with titles that won't fall into the category of unfair competition.

Another area not protected by copyright is the *idea*. This includes musical and lyrical ideas. There have been thousands of songs with lyrics about a man getting drunk in a bar because his woman left him (or vice versa). Each writer who expresses that idea has a copyright in his particular expression of it.

COPYRIGHT INFRINGEMENT

My experience in meeting with songwriters early in their careers is that one of their major concerns revolves around the fear of copyright infringement.

On the one hand, the rookie songwriter is concerned that he will accidentally copy another songwriter's copyrighted work, while on the other hand, he is concerned that someone else will steal the melody or lyrics of one of his compositions.

Before we begin to dwell on these fearful thoughts, let's first find out what copyright infringement actually is, or rather, what the two common kinds of copyright infringement actually are.

The unauthorized use of a copyrighted work is one type of infringement. For example, if a recording of a copyrighted song is released and no royalties are paid to the copyright owner as required by law, the parties releasing and selling the record can be found guilty of copyright infringement. The owner of an establishment where copyrighted songs are performed in public without permission from the copyright owners or their affiliated performing rights societies is also guilty of copyright infringement. [See "Performance Royalties," p. 61.]

The other kind of copyright infringement is the kind I have found young songwriters to be worried about—the copying of substantial portions of a work that is protected by copyright law.

Dozens of times young songwriters have asked me, "How many measures of a song can someone copy without being guilty of copyright infringement?" I'm sorry to have to report that there is no law that stipulates the exact point at which a songwriter has crossed into the area of "substantial similarity." The best way of dealing with this issue is to be original. Don't copy any measures of someone else's song and you won't have to worry so much about the possibility of infringement.

Of course, the other reason songwriters ask this question is because they feel another party is guilty of infringing one of their original works. This brings up another major point about copyright infringement: For there to be infringement, first there has to be proof of access.

For there to be infringement, first there has to be proof of access.

For instance, let's say Bob is a songwriter living in Alaska and Ray is a songwriter living in Alabama. Bob writes a song and makes a demo of it in May. In June, Ray writes a song that is substantially similar to Bob's song.

A copyright exists when a work is put down in a fixed form [see p. 37 for a definition of "fixed"]. Therefore, since Bob's copyright became effective in May, Bob has grounds to sue Ray for copyright infringement, right? Wrong!

Why not? Because Ray had no *access* to Bob's song. If he had no way to hear it, he had no way to copy a substantial portion of it (or any of it, for that matter). Therefore, both Bob and Ray have each created individual copyrightable works.

Let's change the story slightly: Bob writes a song in May and sends it to his cousin Joanne in Alabama. Ray goes to a party at Joanne's house where she is playing Bob's song on a cassette deck. Ray goes home and writes a song, substantially copying Bob's song. Ray figures that Bob's never going to know. He's thousands of miles away.

A few months later a major star records Ray's song (or rather, Ray's rewrite of Bob's song). Bob hears the song on the radio, does a little investigating, and soon Bob and Ray are in court. Because the songs are substantially similar, and because Ray had access to Bob's song, Ray is found guilty of copyright infringement (unless, of course, Ray has a very powerful attorney, in which case anything can happen).

Let's change the story one more time: Bob writes a song that becomes a major hit. Ray is also a successful songwriter. Ten years after Bob's song is a hit, Ray writes a song that is substantially similar melodically, but the lyrics are totally different. Ray's song also becomes a big hit. Bob sues Ray for copyright infringement. Ray argues that the similarity between the two songs is strictly a coincidence. He is a successful songwriter and has no need or desire to intentionally copy Bob's melody. In fact, he has no recollection of ever hearing Bob's song. Is Ray found guilty of copyright infringement? After all, there doesn't seem to be any way to prove Ray had access to Bob's song.

The answer is that Ray is guilty (assuming the powerful attorney was unavailable). Since Bob's song was a major hit, no evidence is required to show how Ray gained access to Bob's song. Even if the song had been a minor hit, access is implied since the song was widely disseminated to the public. Regarding the fact that Ray obviously copied Bob's melody, the question of whether the copying was done consciously or "subconsciously" does not negate the fact that Ray is guilty.

As you can now surmise, copyright infringement is more than a matter of how many measures of one song are similar to another song. If you are still concerned about someone copying a song you've written, the precautionary measure you should take is obvious: Keep track of whoever you send your demo tapes to. Without proof that someone had access to your song, you can't prove that he or she copied it.

Beyond that, your major concern should be to write songs that are original enough so that other people won't accuse you of copying their songs.

Keep track of whoever you send your demo tapes to. Without proof that someone had access to your song, you can't prove that he or she copied it.

PUBLISHING AGREEMENTS AND PUBLISHED SONGS

Now that you've learned a lot about U.S. copyright law, it's time to dig deeper into the definition of music publishing. Consider the following scenario:

Nancy Novice has written a pop song that she feels certain will become better known than the national anthem if she can just get it signed to the right music publisher. Nancy's aunt knows someone who has a cousin in the music business. After a few phone calls, Nancy is sitting across the desk from a real live music publishing executive named Harry Hopeful. Harry listens to Nancy's song, whips out a contract, and says, "Sign here and your song will be signed to Harry Hopeful Music, Inc."

Nancy signs the contract, goes home and tells all of her friends that she just got her first song published. Everyone congratulates her on her success. Parties are thrown, telegrams are sent, and all of Nancy's friends are talking about how famous Nancy is about to become.

Nancy sits back and waits for the money to start rolling in. Days pass and nothing happens. After a few weeks her friends stop asking her about how well her song is doing. A couple of months pass, and finally Nancy calls Harry Hopeful to find out why it's taking so long for her "published song" to become a hit.

Harry replies, "Well, the song is really good, but I haven't found the right artist to record it yet. These things take time."

"I thought our agreement said that you were publishing my song," whines Nancy.

"Oh, you misunderstood," Harry says. "There's a big difference between signing a publishing contract and having a song published."

So what's the difference? For the answer let's go back to the Copyright Act's definition of publication. A song isn't published until there has been "distribution of copies or phonorecords of a work to the public by sale . . ." or an "offering to distribute copies or phonorecords to a group of persons for purposes of further distribution, public performance, or public display."

When Nancy signed a publishing contract with Harry Hopeful Music, Inc., she was giving Harry *permission* to publish her song.

Unless there was a specific clause in her contract stating that Harry had to have sheet music printed and distributed within a specific amount of time (a clause that once existed in contracts during the days when sheet music was the major source of publishing income), Harry was under no obligation to actually "publish" the song.

Obviously, if Harry is a reputable music publisher, he is going to make every effort to get the song recorded by someone. And once the song is recorded and distributed (or there has been an "offering to distribute"), then the song will be a published work.

Until actions have taken place that fulfill the requirements of the Copyright Act's definition of publication, a song isn't published. In Nancy's case, she should have told everyone that her song had been *signed* to a music publisher. After all, that sounds pretty impressive too.

MUSIC PUBLISHING AND THE MUSIC INDUSTRY

Music publishing—although a vital part of the entertainment industry—has, until recently, taken a back seat to some of the more glamorous aspects of the music business. Perhaps it's the intangibility of the publishing industry that caused it to be looked down upon by record companies and other segments of the industry.

Another probable cause of its former lack of appeal was the old image of the crude, cigar-chewing music publisher taking advantage of gullible and naive songwriters.

The real cause of the industry's attitude was probably a lack of understanding of what publishing is all about. Ignorance always tends to breed suspicion.

These negative attitudes have begun to reverse themselves in recent years as the prices publishing catalogs have begun to bring in the marketplace make the real value of music publishing obvious.

Acquisitions and mergers in the publishing industry have shown that there are millions of dollars to be made. Since the music business is a *business*, the fact that music publishing companies are valuable assets has prompted newfound respect among the other elements that make up the entertainment industry.

Major movie studios, record companies, management firms, booking agencies,

A PERSONAL OPINION OF THE SONG SHARK

In the scenario between Nancy Novice and Harry Hopeful I said, "If Harry Hopeful is a reputable music publisher, he is going to make every effort to get [Nancy's] song recorded by someone." Anyone who has been involved in the music business for more than a few days is aware that there are some *dis*reputable music publishers out there as well. Although there are varying degrees of sleaziness within this disreputable lot, none are worse than those known as "song sharks."

Elsewhere in this book, Songwriters Guild of America president George David Weiss comments on the need for songwriters to be protected from "people out there who are constantly seeking to take advantage" of them. He states that songwriters have "an almost desperate need" to have their songs heard. "This desperation," he says, "makes a writer fair game for the song shark. . . ."

A song shark is a person who charges songwriters money for his services. These sharks place advertisements in practically every kind of magazine in America, promising the very things unsuspecting songwriters want to be told. You may have seen ads in which claims are made that the advertiser will add music to your poem or lyrics and make a "professional demo." Such advertisements are schemes that usually result in nothing more than a bad piano/vocal demo for which the songwriter was charged an exorbitant fee. The only person who prospers from this type of venture is the song shark himself.

About twenty years ago I learned about song sharks and decided to see just how reprehensible they could be. One day I sat down and wrote some really atrocious lyrics. Then I looked through the classified ads of a popular magazine and found the section headed "Songwriters." I picked an advertisement that had been placed by a "music publishing company" I'd never heard of before. This particular ad didn't mention money. It simply promised an evaluation of my work. So, I sent my lyrics to the "publishing company" and waited to see what would happen.

A few days later I got a letter back telling me that said company was very excited about my work. There was even a list of what this company claimed were the best lyrics they had received in the past year. There sat my song, right in the top five titles listed. After I got through laughing, I read the rest of the letter. For "only $850" (and this was in the mid-1970s) this company promised to become my publisher, add music to my lyrics and make a demo of the resultant song. There were also the usual promises of airplay, a possible hit, fame, and so on.

Luckily I knew most of these promises were—to be polite—falsehoods. Needless to say, I didn't respond to the letter. Unfortunately, however, many people do. What usually happens is something like this: After the "professional demo" is made, the song shark contacts the songwriter and suggests that a "master recording" be made (for a much higher fee, of course). Then there is money needed to press a thousand copies of the record. After that, there is money needed to promote the record. In some cases the song shark is even able to convince the more gullible of his clients to send more lyrics and keep this process going, always promising that a hit record is right around the corner.

In the end, thousands upon thousands of dollars can be spent before the songwriter discovers that nothing is ever going to happen to further his music career. The truth is, reputable people in the music business just don't do business this way and will have nothing to do with those who carry on such operations.

The key things to know are: 1) Real music publishers do not charge money to sign your song. Usually they pay *you* money in the form of an advance. 2) Real music publishers don't charge you a fee to make a demo. Some may take the cost of the demo out of your future royalties, but no money should ever come out of your pocket to make a demo for a song being signed to a publisher. 3) There's no such thing as a mail-order hit. In my opinion, a real music publisher would never solicit songs through the classified section of a magazine. Publishers get so many tapes every day that there would be no logical reason to be begging for more from the public at large.

There is no lower form of human life than the person who would take advantage of someone in a helpless situation. In my book, the song shark qualifies as one of the lowest forms of human life imaginable.

promotion companies and lots of performers have gone out of business, sold for low figures or gone bankrupt. Music publishing companies, due to their "product," would be hard pressed to go bankrupt.

It's a fascinating fact, but it's true. Why? Because copyrights have extremely long life spans. As long as a song is on a recording that is still selling copies, is being performed on radio or television, is being used in a film or is being sold in sheet music or folio form, royalties are being earned by the publisher of that song. In fact, a song that may be earning only a few pennies a year can suddenly begin earning hundreds of thousands of dollars if it is recorded by an important artist or used in a nationally broadcast commercial.

For example, a song from the 1950s that was an obscure "B" side of a hit single may not have earned any royalties since that original hit dropped off the charts. If that same song from that "B" side is used in a film or recorded by a major artist today, it can gain a whole new life, which will cause it to earn royalties for years to come. I have seen it happen dozens of times with one publishing company that specializes in songs from the early days of Rock & Roll.

For record companies the overhead can be extremely high. There are often many employees to pay; product has to be manufactured; thousands of dollars have to be spent in promotion and advertising. The cost of an unsuccessful album can sometimes bring a record company to its knees.

Meanwhile, the cost to the music publisher of a song on that unsuccessful recording may be no more than the advance paid to the songwriter and an inexpensive demo. And even though the song may not earn back the songwriter's advance on that particular recording, another recording of the same song by another artist on a different label might sell a million copies.

The publisher and the songwriter have the potential to make serious money, while the record company that released the original recording of the song is now stuck with thousands of compact discs and cassettes sitting in a warehouse somewhere.

THE MONEY ISSUE

There is a great deal of money to be made in music publishing. Your knowledge of how that money is earned will give you the chance to see to it that more of it goes into your pocket than into someone else's.

If you are the type of songwriter who writes songs only because you want to create great music (and I hope that's your first priority), you may be turned off by all this talk of money.

The reason I am emphasizing the money aspects of music publishing is because songwriting might one day become your livelihood (if it isn't already). There is a great deal of money to be made in music publishing. Your knowledge of how that money is earned will give you the chance to see to it that more of it goes into your pocket than into someone else's.

Although most successful songwriters became so because their goal was to write good songs, I have discovered that almost all songwriters are prolific for a limited amount of time. I have known songwriters whose biggest hits were written in the 1930s, and others who had a string of hits in the 1960s. Very few writers (if any) have been prolific from the 1930s through the 1990s. The point is, once your period of greatest success is behind you, your income is going to be subject to the agreements you signed at the time. So, although the song should certainly be the most important thing to a songwriter, his business affairs should rank a close second.

Three
SECURING A COPYRIGHT

*O*ne of the most frequently asked questions among newer songwriters is "How do I copyright my song?" The answer might not be what they expect. Many people assume that their song doesn't receive copyright protection until they have filled out a form and sent it to the Copyright Office. Under the 1976 Copyright Act, however, a copyright exists as soon as your song is written down, recorded or otherwise "fixed." Let's go back to the copyright act for another definition:

> A work is "fixed" in a tangible medium of expression when its embodiment in a copy or phonorecord, by or under the authority of the author, is sufficiently permanent or stable to permit it to be perceived, reproduced, or otherwise communicated for a period of more than transitory duration. A work consisting of sounds, images, or both, that are being transmitted, is "fixed" for purposes of this title if a fixation of the work is being made simultaneously with its transmission.

The first thing you learn from this definition is that it's not a good idea to write your songs in disappearing ink. The bottom line here is that once you begin to write your song down on paper or record it in some manner, copyright protection is there. No forms are required to be filled out.

In fact, the law says, "Copyright protection *subsists* . . . in original works of authorship fixed in any tangible medium of expression. . . ." In other words, as you write down or record each note, copyright protection is taking effect. It is a rare occasion when a writer sits down and creates three verses, a bridge and a chorus all at one time. Sometimes it takes days, weeks, months or longer to finish a song. No matter what stage of completion your song has reached, that portion you have "fixed" on paper, tape or other medium is already protected by copyright.

The law also says that if an original song not previously "fixed" is being transmitted (such as in the case of a live broadcast over radio or television), and the song's author is allowing the transmission to be recorded, then a copyright exists by virtue of the fact that the song has been "fixed" under the definition given above.

A copyright exists as soon as your song is written down, recorded or otherwise "fixed."

HOW TO REGISTER A COPYRIGHT

Now that you know your copyright is protected whether you register it or not, the next obvious question is "Why should I bother to register my copyright and pay twenty bucks if it's already protected under law?"

One important reason is that registration allows potential users of your songs to acquire information from the Copyright Office regarding copyright ownership of those works. Of course, there are other sources for this information such as BMI, ASCAP or the Harry Fox Agency as we will discuss later. But there are other important reasons for registration.

In chapter two we addressed the subject of copyright infringement. As you now know, certain situations could arise that would prompt you to bring a lawsuit against someone who you feel is guilty of infringement. Before you can take any legal action on a work originating in the United States, a copyright has to be registered with the Copyright Office. If someone infringes one of your songs, you may sue. If that party is found guilty of willful infringement, you could be entitled to statutory damages of up to $100,000.

There are other legal reasons to register your copyrights that a good lawyer could spend hours explaining to you. The fact is, registration of your copyrights with the Copyright Office is always a good idea.

Registration of a copyright becomes effective when the Copyright Office receives your Form PA, check and copy of the work in the mail. Form PA is the application form created by the Copyright Office for the registration of works that fall into the category of Performing Arts. Several different forms have been devised for registration of copyrightable works, but the one used by songwriters and music publishers is Form PA.

Filling out Form PA is a relatively simple procedure. However, if you don't fill it out exactly as the Copyright Office requires, it will be returned to you with a note explaining what you've omitted or filled out incorrectly. Since it can sometimes take months for your form to be approved and assigned a PA number, it's best to fill it out properly the first time, rather than have to fix your mistakes and wait several more months.

As you can see in the sample Form PA (on pp. 39-40), I have filled out the form using a fictional song title as the work to be registered and using my name as author of the work. Now let's go through the nine sections of Form PA, using this sample as our guide.

1. The first section covers the title of the work, any "Previous or Alternative Titles," and the nature of the work. I have entitled the song "She Lied, I Cried," so that's what I've written on line one.

   Under "Previous or Alternative Titles" I have listed the alternate name of my song as "He Lied, I Cried." It's inevitable that, should my song become a big hit, both genders will want to sing it. By listing this obvious alternative title, it will be much easier for someone searching for the registration to find my song even if they only know it by its alternative title.

   The last line of section 1, "Nature of This Work," is simple. My song consists of both words and music, so the proper description is "Words and Music." If my song had been an instrumental piece, I would have written "Music" on this

FORM PA
For a Work of the Performing Arts
UNITED STATES COPYRIGHT OFFICE

REGISTRATION NUMBER

PA   PAU

EFFECTIVE DATE OF REGISTRATION

Month   Day   Year

DO NOT WRITE ABOVE THIS LINE. IF YOU NEED MORE SPACE, USE A SEPARATE CONTINUATION SHEET.

1

TITLE OF THIS WORK ▼

SHE LIED, I CRIED

PREVIOUS OR ALTERNATIVE TITLES ▼

HE LIED, I CRIED

NATURE OF THIS WORK ▼ See instructions

WORDS AND MUSIC

2

NOTE

Under the law, the "author" of a "work made for hire" is generally the employer, not the employee (see instructions). For any part of this work that was "made for hire" check "Yes" in the space provided, give the employer (or other person for whom the work was prepared) as "Author" of that part, and leave the space for dates of birth and death blank.

a **NAME OF AUTHOR ▼**
WILLIAM RANDALL POE

DATES OF BIRTH AND DEATH
Year Born ▼ 1955   Year Died ▼

Was this contribution to the work a "work made for hire"?
☐ Yes
☒ No

AUTHOR'S NATIONALITY OR DOMICILE
Name of Country
OR { Citizen of ▶ U. S. A.
Domiciled in ▶

WAS THIS AUTHOR'S CONTRIBUTION TO THE WORK
Anonymous? ☐ Yes ☒ No
Pseudonymous? ☐ Yes ☒ No
If the answer to either of these questions is "Yes," see detailed instructions.

NATURE OF AUTHORSHIP Briefly describe nature of material created by this author in which copyright is claimed. ▼
WORDS AND MUSIC

b **NAME OF AUTHOR ▼**

DATES OF BIRTH AND DEATH
Year Born ▼   Year Died ▼

Was this contribution to the work a "work made for hire"?
☐ Yes
☐ No

AUTHOR'S NATIONALITY OR DOMICILE
Name of Country
OR { Citizen of ▶
Domiciled in ▶

WAS THIS AUTHOR'S CONTRIBUTION TO THE WORK
Anonymous? ☐ Yes ☐ No
Pseudonymous? ☐ Yes ☐ No
If the answer to either of these questions is "Yes," see detailed instructions.

NATURE OF AUTHORSHIP Briefly describe nature of material created by this author in which copyright is claimed. ▼

c **NAME OF AUTHOR ▼**

DATES OF BIRTH AND DEATH
Year Born ▼   Year Died ▼

Was this contribution to the work a "work made for hire"?
☐ Yes
☐ No

AUTHOR'S NATIONALITY OR DOMICILE
Name of Country
OR { Citizen of ▶
Domiciled in ▶

WAS THIS AUTHOR'S CONTRIBUTION TO THE WORK
Anonymous? ☐ Yes ☐ No
Pseudonymous? ☐ Yes ☐ No
If the answer to either of these questions is "Yes," see detailed instructions.

NATURE OF AUTHORSHIP Briefly describe nature of material created by this author in which copyright is claimed. ▼

3

a **YEAR IN WHICH CREATION OF THIS WORK WAS COMPLETED** This information must be given in all cases. ◀ Year
1997

b **DATE AND NATION OF FIRST PUBLICATION OF THIS PARTICULAR WORK** Complete this information ONLY if this work has been published.
Month ▶   Day ▶   Year ▶   ◀ Nation

4

See instructions before completing this space.

COPYRIGHT CLAIMANT(S) Name and address must be given even if the claimant is the same as the author given in space 2. ▼

a
WILLIAM RANDALL POE
461 OCEAN BOULEVARD
MALIBU, CA 98765-4321

TRANSFER If the claimant(s) named here in space 4 is (are) different from the author(s) named in space 2, give a brief statement of how the claimant(s) obtained ownership of the copyright. ▼

b

APPLICATION RECEIVED

ONE DEPOSIT RECEIVED

TWO DEPOSITS RECEIVED

FUNDS RECEIVED

DO NOT WRITE HERE OFFICE USE ONLY

MORE ON BACK ▶
• Complete all applicable spaces (numbers 5-9) on the reverse side of this page.
• See detailed instructions.
• Sign the form at line 8.

DO NOT WRITE HERE
Page 1 of _____ pages

EXAMINED BY		FORM PA
CHECKED BY		
☐ CORRESPONDENCE Yes		FOR COPYRIGHT OFFICE USE ONLY

DO NOT WRITE ABOVE THIS LINE. IF YOU NEED MORE SPACE, USE A SEPARATE CONTINUATION SHEET.

PREVIOUS REGISTRATION Has registration for this work, or for an earlier version of this work, already been made in the Copyright Office?

☐ Yes ☒ No   If your answer is "Yes," why is another registration being sought? (Check appropriate box) ▼

a. ☐ This is the first published edition of a work previously registered in unpublished form.

b. ☐ This is the first application submitted by this author as copyright claimant.

c. ☐ This is a changed version of the work, as shown by space 6 on this application.

If your answer is "Yes," give: **Previous Registration Number** ▼   **Year of Registration** ▼

5

DERIVATIVE WORK OR COMPILATION   Complete both space 6a and 6b for a derivative work; complete only 6b for a compilation.

a. Preexisting Material Identify any preexisting work or works that this work is based on or incorporates. ▼

b. Material Added to This Work Give a brief, general statement of the material that has been added to this work and in which copyright is claimed. ▼

6

See instructions
before completing
this space.

DEPOSIT ACCOUNT If the registration fee is to be charged to a Deposit Account established in the Copyright Office, give name and number of Account.
Name ▼   **Account Number** ▼

a

7

CORRESPONDENCE Give name and address to which correspondence about this application should be sent.   Name/Address/Apt/City/State/ZIP ▼

WILLIAM RANDALL POE
461 OCEAN BOULEVARD
MALIBU, CA 98765-4321

b

Area Code and Daytime Telephone Number ▶ (310) 555-1234   Fax Number ▶ (310) 555-4321

CERTIFICATION* I, the undersigned, hereby certify that I am the

Check only one ▼

☒ author

☐ other copyright claimant

☐ owner of exclusive right(s)

☐ authorized agent of _____
Name of author or other copyright claimant, or owner of exclusive right(s) ▲

8

of the work identified in this application and that the statements made
by me in this application are correct to the best of my knowledge.

Typed or printed name and date ▼ If this application gives a date of publication in space 3, do not sign and submit it before that date.

WILLIAM RANDALL POE   Date ▶ 9/22/97

👉   Handwritten signature (X) ▼

William Randall Poe

Mail certificate to:	Name ▼ WILLIAM RANDALL POE	YOU MUST: • Complete all necessary spaces • Sign your application in space 8	**9**
	Number/Street/Apt ▼	SEND ALL 3 ELEMENTS IN THE SAME PACKAGE:	
Certificate will be mailed in window envelope	461 OCEAN BOULEVARD	1. Application form 2. Nonrefundable $20 filing fee in check or money order payable to *Register of Copyrights* 3. Deposit material	
	City/State/ZIP ▼ MALIBU, CA 98765-4321	MAIL TO: Register of Copyrights Library of Congress Washington, D.C. 20559-6000	

*17 U.S.C. § 506(e): Any person who knowingly makes a false representation of a material fact in the application for copyright registration provided for by section 409, or in any written statement filed in connection with the application, shall be fined not more than $2,500.

September 1995—400,000   ♲ PRINTED ON RECYCLED PAPER   ☆U.S. GOVERNMENT PRINTING OFFICE: 1995-387-237/20,024 line. If I had only written lyrics for which no melody had yet been composed, I would have written the phrase "Song Lyrics." You get the idea.

2. The second section of the form requires information about the author(s) of the work. The Copyright Office wants "the fullest form of the author's name," so I've written William Randall Poe. Under "Dates of Birth and Death" I have listed the year I was born. Luckily, I get to leave the other half blank. If, in fact, a Form PA was being filled out for a song by a deceased writer, it would be necessary to list the year of death so that the length of copyright protection could be properly determined.

In chapter two in the section entitled "The Copyright Owner," we learned that a "work made for hire" is "a work prepared by an employee within the scope of his or her employment" or a work commissioned from one of the nine "work made for hire" categories listed on p. 27. My song is not a work made for hire, so I have checked "No."

Next comes "Author's Nationality or Domicile." I've written "U.S.A." on the appropriate line. Since I want everyone to know I wrote "She Lied, I Cried," my work is neither anonymous nor pseudonymous, so I've checked "No" in both boxes.

However, had I wished to remain anonymous, I would have checked the "Yes" box. Under "Name of Author," as an anonymous writer I would have either: 1) left the line blank; 2) written "Anonymous" on the line; or 3) written my full name, making sure that I had checked "Yes" in the appropriate box. The life of the copyright of an anonymous author has the potential to be much shorter than a copyright in which the true name of the author has been revealed.

If I had written the song using the pseudonym Sammy James, I would have checked "Yes" where indicated on the form. My choices under "Name of Author" would have been to: 1) leave the line blank; 2) write my pseudonym and indicate it as such ("Sammy James, pseudonym"); or 3) write my real name and my pseudonym, making sure I had clearly shown which was which ("William Randall Poe, whose pseudonym is Sammy James"). Once again, in certain circumstances I could be shortening the life of the copyright if I used a pseudonym. Whether I had decided to use a pseudonym or remain anonymous, I would still have to list my citizenship or domicile.

The last line of section 2a is "Nature of Authorship." Since I wrote the song by myself, I put "Words and Music" here. If I had written just the words and someone else had composed the music, my line would say "Words" and my co-writer's line would say "Music." If both of us had contributed to the lyrics and melody of the song, we would each be listed as "Co-Author of Words and Music."

3. The third section of Form PA involves creation and publication. We already know that a copyright is created when it's "fixed" for the first time in a copy or a phonorecord. In the case of my song, I recorded the music on a cassette in 1995 and wrote the lyrics in 1997. Since I am registering the completed version of my song, I have written 1997 as the year of creation.

My song hasn't been published yet (otherwise my publisher would probably be filling out this form instead of me), so I left the "first publication" section blank. At the beginning of chapter two, we learned what constitutes a published

The life of the copyright of an anonymous author has the potential to be much shorter than a copyright in which the true name of the author has been revealed.

work. If, say, a commercial recording of my song had been distributed beginning on February 1, 1997 that would be the date listed as "First Publication of This Particular Work." Assuming this was initially a domestic release, the "Nation of First Publication" would be "U.S.A."

4. Section 4 requires the name and address of the "Copyright Claimant(s)." Since I wrote the song alone and have not assigned, sold or transferred it to another party, I have listed my own name and address. Under "Transfer" I have left the line blank.

   If I had signed an agreement with a music publisher for "She Lied, I Cried," the publisher would, in most cases, be listed as the Copyright Claimant, and the words "By written contract" (or a similar phrase) would be listed under "Transfer."

5. Section 5 pertains to any "Previous Registration" of the copyright. On my application I've checked "No" because this is my first registration of the song. The reasons why there would be a need for registering the copyright a second time include listing an additional author as a copyright claimant or registering a "changed version of the work."

   Earlier I said that I had written the music to my song in 1995 and added the lyrics in 1997. If I had registered the copyright when it was still an instrumental piece, I would now need to register the work again because it would fall into the category of a "changed version of the work."

6. The sixth section is for songs that are derivative works or compilations or for a song that is a "changed version." I have left this section blank because it doesn't pertain to my song. If the melody to "She Lied, I Cried" had been partially based on the tune of Offenbach's Barcarolle in D Major from the opera *Les Contes d'Hoffman*, I would have indicated that fact on line 6a. On the line for 6b I would have written "New words added; revision of melody."

7. The first half of section 7 is for those who register copyrights so frequently that they have established a "Deposit Account" with the Copyright Office. Once again, I have left the first half of this section blank since I don't have an account. Instead, I will send a check for twenty dollars along with the application and a cassette containing a recording of "She Lied, I Cried." If I want to, I could send a lead sheet of the song instead of a tape.

   The second half of section 7 is for "Correspondence" purposes. For a variety of reasons (including if I have filled out this application incorrectly, or if I forgot to include my check or my tape), the Copyright Office needs to know how to contact me.

8. Next comes section 8 regarding "Certification," in which I have certified that I am the copyright claimant by checking "author." I have also typed my name and the date, and have signed the application on the appropriate line.

9. Finally, section 9 is for the name and address of the person to whom the certificate

should be mailed. Once the Copyright Office has processed your Form PA, it will be assigned a number and returned to you.

REGISTERING SEVERAL SONGS AT ONCE

Now that you know how to register one song using Form PA, it's time for me to let you in on a relatively little-known secret for saving money by registering several songs at a time. After all, if you're a prolific songwriter with dozens of songs to register, the process of registering them one at a time can become a pretty expensive enterprise. And the Copyright Office doesn't offer volume discounts!

The fee for registering Form PA is currently twenty dollars*. By filing another document called Form CA for an additional twenty dollars, you can register several songs at once. If you'd rather pay forty bucks instead of four hundred bucks to register twenty songs, here's the trick:

On Form PA, rather than listing one song on the "Title of This Work" line, write a phrase that describes the group of songs you wish to register. For instance, if I have twelve songs to register, I can entitle my work "A Dozen by Randy Poe, Volume One." Any phrase that describes the collection will do: "Songs from the Winter of 1998," "Forty Love Songs," "Songs Written on the 'A' Train While Commuting to Work." The idea is to give your group of songs a collective title.

When you register an unpublished song, you must include a lead sheet or cassette of the work. When registering a collection of songs, you should either: 1) make a cassette that contains all of the songs in the collection or 2) put all of the lead sheets in the collection in an orderly manner by either fastening them together or binding them in a folder.

Any time something seems less expensive than it should be, there are usually a few strings attached. This method of registering a collection of songs is no exception. To be able to register more than one song on Form PA, all of the songs must: 1) have the same copyright claimant or claimants and 2) be by the same author; or, if there is more than one author, at least one author has to have written part of each of the songs in the collection. If your songs still qualify, then your next step is to mail in your Form PA with the appropriate materials and wait for your registration certificate to return.

Once it arrives, you will have a PA number and you'll be ready for part two: Form CA. The "CA" stands for "Correction/Amplification." The purpose of filing this form is to amplify the information given on your Form PA.

On Form CA you will need to write the title of your collection, the Form PA registration number and the year of basic registration, as well as the author's or authors' name(s) and the name(s) of the copyright claimant(s). Under the section for "Amplified Information," you will list all of the individual song titles that make up your collection. When Form CA is being used to amplify a Form PA, the same person who signed the PA must also sign the CA form.

When you've completed Form CA, send it to the Copyright Office along with

---

*The only things certain in life are death, taxes and the fact that the cost of registering a copyright will continue to escalate. Read the copyright form carefully and make sure you know the current cost of registration before you send in the form. Otherwise, it'll be winging its way back to you faster than you can say "budget crisis."

twenty dollars, and you will have successfully registered an entire collection of songs for a total of forty bucks. When they receive your Form CA, the Copyright Office will cross-reference the collection with the titles of the songs listed on the form, which is the equivalent of having registered each song individually. The money you save will go a long way toward making that next demo.

HOW TO GET COPIES OF FORMS PA AND CA

Now that you know how to fill out Forms PA and CA, you'll need a few of your own. If you aren't shy around phone answering machines, you can get forms quickly by calling the Copyright Office Hotline at (202)707-9100.

When you call you'll get an answering machine that will instruct you to leave your name and address, and the type and number of forms you want. Be sure to speak slowly and spell anything that might be easily misspelled. You can order more than one form at a time, but it's best to order only the amount you need, plus a few extras for additional songs you may wish to register in the near future. My experience with the Hotline is that the response time is very quick. I have frequently received forms within three days of the time I ordered them.

You can also order circulars put out by the Copyright Office using the Hotline number. Circular 1 is entitled "Copyright Basics"; Circular 4 tells the latest "Copyright Fees"; Circular 9 explains "Work-Made-For-Hire Under the 1976 Copyright Act"—in true government fashion, the list goes on forever. Luckily, the Copyright Office also has a site on the Internet, so many of the circulars can be downloaded for your reading enjoyment. (I know what you're thinking, and the answer is: no, it's not copyright infringement to download government documents.)

If you don't like dealing with answering machines, and if the Internet isn't your cup of tea, you can always write the Copyright Office at the following address, requesting the forms and circulars you need:

Information and Publications Section, LM-455
Copyright Office
Library of Congress
Washington, DC 20559-6000

Four

ROYALTIES FOR SONGWRITERS AND PUBLISHERS

*T*his section of the book could more precisely be called "The Money Chapter." It's time to put away those "root of all evil" feelings that may still be lurking in your conscience and accept the fact that one of the primary functions of a music publisher is to turn a healthy profit. The two main reasons I have written this book are to teach you about the business of music publishing and to help you—as a songwriter—make at least (or, at the very least, almost) as much money on your songs as your publisher will.

This chapter and the one to follow will fill you in on all of the major ways music publishers and songwriters receive income: mechanical royalties, synchronization royalties, performance royalties, royalties for grand rights, print royalties, royalties from something called "new media," and royalties from foreign sources.

Having read the first three chapters, some of these terms are probably beginning to sound familiar to you. Slowly but surely, you're learning the language of the music publishing business.

You—as a songwriter—should make at least or almost as much money on your songs as your publisher will.

MECHANICAL ROYALTIES

Mechanical royalties are monies paid by a record company for the right to manufacture and distribute phonorecords containing a song owned by the publisher. The amount of money to be paid per unit is usually either the current statutory mechanical rate, or a "reduced rate" negotiated by the record company and the music publisher, generally based on a percentage of the statutory mechanical rate.

Okay, I know I've thrown in a bunch of new terms in the course of a couple of sentences, so here go a few definitions and explanations:

First, by now the word phonorecords has popped up enough times that you know it means such things as compact discs, audiotapes and records, as well as any similar devices that are created in the future.

Second, the phrase "per unit" refers to the total number of phonorecords in question. If a record company manufactures and distributes ten thousand compact discs and five thousand cassettes, the total number of units is fifteen thousand. (Anything more complicated would require me to use a calculator.)

Third, the "statutory mechanical rate" is the amount of money that the record company owes the music publisher for each unit manufactured and distributed as long as no "reduced rate" has been agreed to by the two parties.

In chapter two you learned that a compulsory mechanical license was originally created under the 1909 Copyright Act and expanded upon in the 1976 law. This license gives companies that wish to reproduce songs mechanically the right to do so without having to obtain the permission of the copyright owner as long as phonorecords of the song have previously been distributed to the public in the United States under the copyright owner's authority. The compulsory mechanical license rules regarding royalty payments require the record company to make those payments on a monthly basis, provide monthly accountings "under oath," and pay the statutory mechanical rate based on the number of phonorecords manufactured and distributed.

A *negotiated* mechanical license is a variation on the compulsory mechanical license. Generally known in the music industry simply as a "mechanical license," this license is more lenient than a compulsory mechanical license, usually requiring payments on a quarterly basis (as opposed to monthly), sometimes causing payments to be made only on phonorecords sold (as opposed to the total amount of recordings manufactured and distributed), and sometimes allowing for a reduced rate (as opposed to the statutory mechanical rate). A compulsory mechanical license doesn't require permission from the copyright owner to manufacture and distribute records, but a negotiated mechanical license does by virtue of the fact that the license is being negotiated between the record company and the copyright owner.

A mechanical license, then, is a negotiated license allowing a particular record company permission to manufacture and distribute a recording that contains a song owned by a particular music publisher without having to follow the strict guidelines of a compulsory (nonnegotiable) mechanical license.

When the 1976 Copyright Act was created, a five-person panel called the Copyright Royalty Tribunal (CRT) was put into place. These five people, appointed by the President and confirmed by the Senate, were empowered to (among other things) determine the amount of the statutory mechanical rate.

Since the implementation of the 1976 Copyright Act, the statutory mechanical rate was increased several times over the first decade of the new Law. In 1987, a more detailed mathematical formula for determining the amount of future increases was jointly devised by the National Music Publishers' Association (NMPA), the Songwriters Guild of America (SGA) and the Recording Industry Association of America (RIAA). That formula—based on changes in the Consumer Price Index— was then adopted by the Copyright Royalty Tribunal.

However, as you are quickly learning, the Copyright Law goes through changes seemingly as fast as a baby goes through diapers, because on December 17, 1993, Congress abolished the Copyright Royalty Tribunal, directing the Library of Congress and the Copyright Office to adopt the rules and regulations of the CRT. As instructed, the Copyright Office continued to base the adjustment of the rate on the same formula the CRT had adopted, resulting in the current rate (as of January 1, 1996) of 6.95 cents, or 1.3 cents per minute, whichever is larger.

Interestingly, this rate change for 1996 was the last scheduled adjustment under the rules of the former Copyright Royalty Tribunal. So, you're probably saying to yourself, what's going to happen now? Luckily, the government has an answer for that. Pursuant to Section 803(a)(3) of the U.S. Copyright Act, any owner or user of

"Reduced rate" is a mechanical rate negotiated between a record company and a music publisher (the copyright owner) in which the two parties agree to a lower amount per unit than the amount of the statutory mechanical rate.

a copyrighted musical work affected by the Act's compulsory mechanical licensing provisions can file a petition with the Library of Congress during calendar year 1997, requesting an adjustment of the statutory mechanical rate covering the period from 1998 to 2007. It is very safe to assume that the NMPA, SGA, RIAA and other interested parties will be putting their collective heads together to determine the best possible approach for the future.

Reduced Rate

Now let's get back to our definition of terms. A "reduced rate" is a mechanical rate negotiated between a record company and a music publisher (the copyright owner) in which the two parties agree to a lower amount per unit than the amount of the statutory mechanical rate.

The most common of these reduced amounts is referred to as a "three-quarter rate." What the record company and music publisher are agreeing to in this situation is that the record company will pay 75 percent of the current statutory mechanical rate per unit.

In other words, if the current statutory rate is 6.95 cents, in a reduced rate situation the record company is agreeing to pay 5.2125 cents per unit (or 75 percent of 6.95 cents). Although the three-quarter rate is the most commonly negotiated rate, I have seen instances where the reduced rate is anywhere from 50 to 87.50 percent, depending on the particular situation.

It is usually in the publisher's best interest to negotiate a reduced rate using a percentage instead of a specific amount of money. The reason for this is because the statutory mechanical rate has continued to go up. If, in 1995, a publisher agreed to a reduced rate of "4.95 cents" as opposed to "75 percent of the current statutory rate," the publisher would be making less money on that recording for royalties due on or after January 1, 1996, because the record company would continue to pay only 4.95 cents. Meanwhile, the publisher who negotiated a "three-quarter rate" in 1995 would begin making 5.2125 cents per unit in 1996.

Determination of the amount of the reduced rate (if it is to be reduced at all) is usually based on how badly the record company needs to use the song in relation to how badly the music publisher wants the song to be used.

For example, an artist is in the studio trying to decide between two songs to record. The album needs only one more number to wrap it up, and everyone agrees that either song will be fine. At this point there are several factors to consider: studio time, musicians' fees, arrangement costs, production costs, and so forth.

Now might be a good time for the record company to contact the songs' publishers and see if either of them will grant a reduced rate. If neither of them will, the record company will have to choose some other factor to determine which song to record. (The same problem applies if both publishers agree to a three-quarter rate.) However, if one publisher says yes to a reduced rate and the other doesn't, it's a pretty safe bet that the record company will go with the song belonging to the publisher who grants the reduced rate.

Just look at the numbers: If the statutory rate is 6.95 cents per unit, and the record company manufactures and distributes one million units, the record company will owe the publisher 6.95 cents times one million—a total of $69,500.

On a three-quarter rate basis, using the same million units, the record company owes the publisher $52,125, a savings to the record company of $17,375.

If one publisher says yes to a reduced rate and another doesn't, it's a pretty safe bet that the record company will go with the song belonging to the publisher who grants the reduced rate.

As you can see, the real situation here is that the publisher is forced to make a decision. Unless there are spies filling him in on what's really happening at the record company, in many cases the publisher doesn't know the true reason why the record company is asking for a reduced rate.

The publisher has to ask himself several questions: Will the record company go with another song if I don't grant a reduced rate? If I grant a reduced rate on this song, are my chances better at getting another song I publish on a future album the record company puts out? Do I owe someone at the record company a favor? Is the album already finished and about to be released (in which case the record company is bluffing)? The variations on these questions are almost endless.

You might be surprised to discover that record companies don't always contact the publisher *before* a song is recorded. However, there is a natural battle constantly being fought between the creative forces and the "bean counters" in most record companies.

If an artist wants to record a particular song, that decision might come in a recording studio at two in the morning when there is no record company executive around to say, "Wait! Don't spend $20,000 in studio time and musician costs until we can find out if the publisher will grant a reduced rate."

Another common case of record companies not being in a negotiating position sometimes comes about when a compilation album is being prepared. If a record company plans to put out an album of the fifteen greatest hits of 1957, and I own the publishing rights to one of the top ten songs from that year, I can refuse to grant a reduced rate because it is a relatively safe assumption that my song will have to be included on the album despite the record company's threats to leave it off.

Of course, reason usually prevails among publishers in these situations. Some giant publishing companies will grant a reduced rate at the drop of a hat because they are dealing in such large volume. Smaller publishers tend to be more conservative and cautious. If a publisher has only twenty songs in his catalog, he might have to make a decision that may or may not reduce his company's annual income by a large percentage.

This, then, is one area of publishing that isn't cut and dried. There is actual gamesmanship going on between the record company and the music publisher that can mean a substantial difference in the amount of money one makes and the other doesn't.

There is actual gamesmanship going on between the record company and the music publisher that can mean a substantial difference in the amount of money one makes and the other doesn't.

Enter the Harry Fox Agency

There is a company based in New York City that acts as a licensing organization/collection agency for music publishers. A wholly owned subsidiary of the National Music Publishers' Association, the Harry Fox Agency provides licensing services to thousands of publishers, issuing mechanical licenses to record companies and collecting mechanical royalties on the publishers' behalf.

The agency issues mechanical licenses for which service it charges publishers (and, consequently, songwriters) a commission fee—currently 4½ percent "off the top"—on royalties collected from the record company on the publishers' behalf.

Let's go back to our million unit sales that would earn the publisher a gross of $69,500. A common situation would be for the publisher to pay half of the $69,500 ($34,750) to the songwriter. If the Harry Fox Agency collects the mechanical royal-

THE NATIONAL MUSIC PUBLISHERS' ASSOCIATION (OR, WHO WAS HARRY FOX?)

Originally known as the Music Publishers' Protective Association when it was formed in 1917, the National Music Publishers' Association—NMPA—was founded to protect and advance the interests of music publishers in the United States.

In its early days NMPA began campaigning for changes in the copyright law. Representatives of the organization helped to make up the panel that studied the important changes being proposed in the mid-1950s when Congress began to consider revisions in the 1909 act. As you learned in chapter two, the law was finally revised in 1976, with additional changes taking place in 1989 when the United States joined the Berne Convention (as well as other changes—both major and minor—that have taken place since 1989. To list every single change made in the U.S. copyright law between 1976 and 1996 would fill a book—and it wouldn't be nearly as much fun to read as this one).

As copyrighted music began to be used in films, NMPA created a service that issued synchronization licenses on behalf of all music publishers who wished to use NMPA as their licensing agent. In charge of this service was NMPA's chairman of the board, E. Claude Mills. In 1936, NMPA added licensing electrical transcriptions of radio programs to its list of services to publishers.

Two years later, a gentleman named Harry Fox was given the task of licensing recordings, collecting mechanical royalties and then distributing those royalties to the appropriate publishers, along with continuing the other services NMPA had already instituted.

When Harry Fox died in 1969, the Harry Fox Agency was created as a wholly owned subsidiary of the National Music Publishers' Association. Today the Harry Fox Agency continues to issue synchronization and mechanical licenses on behalf of all music publishers who have entered into agreements with Fox for this service.

The Harry Fox Agency is also involved in other facets of music publishing, including foreign administration [see chapter five]. More information on NMPA and the Harry Fox Agency is available by writing to NMPA/ The Harry Fox Agency, 711 Third Ave., New York, NY 10017. The phone number is (212) 370-5330; fax number is (212) 953-2384.

ties for those million units, it will take a commission fee of $3,127.50 (4½ percent), leaving the publisher with a gross of $66,372.50 from which the writer will be paid $33,186.25 (half of $66,372.50). The publisher and the songwriter each end up with $1,563.75 less than what the record company paid to Fox.

So why doesn't the music publishing company issue its own mechanical licenses and save the 4½ percent? Well, some do. However, a major function of HFA is to conduct audits of record companies all over the country, finding money due to publishers and distributing these "recoveries" to whomever royalties are owed. In its promotional literature, the National Music Publishers' Association points out that, in many cases, the Fox Agency distributes recoveries "in excess of the commission" the publisher pays for Fox's services. As far as granting reduced rates is concerned, the Fox Agency will do so only if the publisher agrees to the request.

Every music publishing company has to decide whether or not using the Harry Fox Agency makes sense financially in its particular case. For larger publishers with thousands of copyrights, many licenses are issued every day. In this case, the Fox Agency may be better equipped to handle this heavy workload, and its commission will probably turn out to be less than the cost to the publisher of hiring additional persons to do this work.

For a smaller company with only a handful of songs, it might make more sense for the publisher to issue licenses himself. However, collecting monies owed from a record company on the other side of the country might become a costly exercise. Auditing that company can be an expensive proposition also.

Once again, every publisher's case is different, and the ultimate decision to be made is whether using the Fox Agency is financially feasible for the publishing company in question.

Mechanical Royalties in Action

So far in this chapter you've learned about the statutory mechanical rate, reduced rates, gamesmanship in the music business, the Harry Fox Agency and mechanical licenses—all of which pertain to one of the main sources of the music publisher's income: mechanical royalties. Now let's set up some scenarios and see how all of these things fit together.

Scenario Number One

Madonna Megastar has just recorded an album's worth of material. Being a prolific songwriter, she has composed eleven of the twelve songs, but the twelfth one is a song owned by Sam's Smalltime Music Publishing Company.

Sam doesn't use the Harry Fox Agency, so Ed Promo, an executive from Ms. Megastar's record company, contacts Sam directly, telling him that the song will be on the album if Sam will grant a three-quarter rate.

Sam knows that Madonna Megastar's last four albums have sold over a million copies each. A little math tells him that 25 percent of 6.95 cents times one million units is $17,375. So, it's up to Sam to decide whether to say yes to the reduced rate and lose a potential additional profit of $17,375, or say no and face the possibility of making nothing at all if the record company replaces his song with somebody else's.

Not owning thousands of copyrights, Sam decides not to gamble and agrees to the three-quarter rate. So, Sam issues a mechanical license to the record company. His license calls for payments for the quarters ending March 31, June 30, September 30 and December 31, just as the Fox Agency's license does.

In the music industry, record companies are usually allowed forty-five days after the end of each quarter to make royalty payments. Since Madonna Megastar is on a major label with a good track record for making proper payments, and since her new album is another big seller, Sam's Smalltime Music Publishing Company is soon reaping the profits produced by the inclusion of the song from Sam's publishing catalog.

Whether or not Sam's song would have been on the album even if he had refused to grant a three-quarter rate is something he may never know. If Ed Promo knew that the song was going to go on the album whether or not Sam granted the rate, he's not likely to tell Sam. That would only encourage Sam to refuse to grant a rate in the future if Ed made the same request for another record that he really needed a reduced rate for.

Besides, the music industry—despite the fact that its actions are felt around the world via hit songs—is a very small community. Experienced executives in the music business know that making enemies is never a good idea. A year from now Sam may be in a powerful position and Ed Promo might be looking for a job. If Sam knows that Ed once took advantage of him, Ed isn't likely to be able to find employment at Sam's Bigtime Music Publishing Company.

Scenario Number Two

Harry Hunk is recording an album of Rock & Roll songs from the 1950s and 1960s. Don Dealer has a publishing company consisting of songs that were hits during that era. As it turns out, three of the songs on Harry's album are published by Don Dealer's publishing company.

Record company executive Rita Rategetter calls Don to give him the good news and to ask for reduced rates on the three tunes. Don's been making deals for a long time. He would prefer not to give reduced rates if he doesn't have to, but Rita has done favors for him in the past, so he agrees to grant a three-quarter rate on all three songs on a "most favored nations" basis. In other words, if all of the other publishers whose songs appear on Harry's album grant reduced rates, Don will too. But, if anyone gets a higher rate, so does Don. "However," Don tells Rita, "you have to agree that one of my songs will be on either the 'A' or 'B' side of any singles released from the album until all three of my songs have been used, and that the mechanical royalties from the singles will be paid at statutory rate."*

Rita agrees to Don's request, which means Don's publishing company will receive mechanical royalties not only on album sales but also on as many as three singles released from the album. Even if Harry Hunk's record company puts out three singles and puts Don Dealer's songs on the "B" sides of those three singles, Don's company will make as much money on mechanical royalties as the publishing companies who own the rights to the songs on the "A" sides.

Later in this chapter we will cover the subject of performance royalties. The "A" side of a single earns more money than the "B" side because performance income is earned on the "A" side (the side that receives airplay). However, the amount of mechanical royalties earned is the same for both sides, assuming that both sides of the recording are being paid the same mechanical rate. To show you

---

* Granted, these days we're mainly dealing in CD and cassette singles. So, when I refer to the "B" side, I mean the song that's not the one the record company is trying to get airplay for. In other words, the "A" side of the single is the one the label wants to become a "hit." The "B" side is there primarily to give the record company an excuse for charging so much for the CD single in the first place.

what Don's earnings from mechanicals can be on the deal he has made with Rita, I've done some multiplication below:

Harry Hunk's album sells 250,000 units. Since there are three songs on the album published by Don Dealer, Don's publishing company gets 5.2125 cents (75 percent of statutory) times 3 times 250,000. This means that Don's company has grossed $39,093.75.

However, since Rita agreed to Don's request about releasing Don's songs on Harry's singles, there are more mechanical royalties for Don to earn—this time at 6.95 cents per unit. The first single sells 50,000 units, the second single sells 75,000 units, and the third single sells 55,000 units. Once again, Don's company gets 6.95 cents per unit, giving Don an additional $12,510 (or 6.95 cents times 180,000) in mechanical income.

Since Don is always thinking about how to make the best deal for his publishing company (and for the writers of the songs Don publishes), he brought his company over $12,500 in extra income.

Scenario Number Three

Linda Lucky has recently started a publishing company in New York City and has already had a couple of hits. Linda gets a license request from the Harry Fox Agency, informing her that a small record company in the Midwest has recorded one of her songs and wants a reduced rate.

Linda realizes that the chances of getting a hit on a small label with an unknown artist are very poor. Since there isn't much money to be made from this release she decides to try to make as much as she can out of the situation and refuses to grant a reduced rate.

The Harry Fox Agency gives this information to the small record company's president, Sid Sneaky. Sid agrees to pay the statutory rate because he really wants to release the record. The Harry Fox Agency issues a mechanical license to Sid's record company. As it turns out, the record becomes a regional hit, selling 30,000 copies.

Several months pass, and Linda Lucky realizes that she hasn't received any mechanical royalties from sneaky Sid. Since Sid's company is over a thousand miles away, it's not feasible for Linda to send her accountant to the Midwest to audit Sid's company, especially since the record didn't sell enough copies to become a national hit.

As luck would have it, several publishers have been complaining to the Harry Fox Agency about lack of payments from Sid Sneaky, so HFA sends an auditor to Sid's company and discovers that he owes thousands of dollars to a host of music publishers. Soon Linda Lucky and the other publishers receive their royalties, thanks to the Fox Agency's efforts.

Mechanical Royalty Earnings

As strange as some of these scenarios may seem, this is everyday life in the music business. Understandably, most record companies want to pay as little as they have to for the use of songs, and most publishers want to make as much money as possible every time one of their songs is used. It is this ongoing, back-and-forth action between licensors and licensees that helps to make the music industry an interesting place to work, even for those who aren't songwriters or performers.

Sampling

In another classic case of inexplicable music business lingo, the word "sampling" actually has more than one meaning in this profession, depending on which area of the music business you're in.

The type of sampling which involves songwriters and music publishers is the kind where part or all of an existing song is used to create another, new song.

Ordinarily this is done by an artist who takes a piece of a pre-existing recording and uses that piece (or "sample") to make a new recording. For example, the chart-topping recording of "Regulate" by Warren G consisted of Mr. G doing a medium-tempo "singing rap" (for lack of a better description) over the keyboard portion of Michael McDonald's recording of "I Keep Forgettin'." In other words, although the lyrics and "melody" of "Regulate" were written by Warren G, a good portion of the actual recording used to make Warren G's record entitled "Regulate" was, in fact, the original recording of Michael McDonald's keyboard performance from McDonald's recording of "I Keep Forgettin'."

In some situations a "sample" might consist of no more than the bass line of a pre-existing recording (or even just a trumpet blast, drum lick, scream, etc.). In others, an entire pre-existing master might be used, with additional lyrics and/or instrumentation added to it. Or the whole chorus of a pre-existing recording might be "stripped into" a new recording.

The above-described examples of samples would be, in most cases, defined as "derivative works." (Which finally leads us to what all of this sampling stuff has to do with mechanical royalties in the first place.)

Since you now know that the right "to prepare derivative works based upon the copyrighted work" is one of the five exclusive rights of the copyright owner (remember "Mary Had a Miniature Infant Sheep, Uh-huh!"?), then you know that if someone else wishes to create a new work based upon your copyrighted work, they must secure the right to do so from you as the owner of the pre-existing copyrighted work.

Usually, how much a music publisher decides to charge for that right (should the publisher decide to grant the use at all) is variable, and is generally based on the extent of the "sample" in question.

For instance, if the bass, rhythm guitar and drum pattern of a pre-existing recording of a song is used by an artist who then creates new lyrics, a new chorus, new background vocals and new horn parts to lay over those three instruments (without using the lyrics of the pre-existing work), then the publisher of the pre-existing song might determine that he should receive 50 percent of the mechanical royalties derived from the new work.

If more of the song is used, the publisher might ask for 75 percent of the mechanical royalties; conversely, if less is used, the percentage could drop considerably. If only a small fraction of the song is used, the publisher might just agree to a "buy-out" (or one-time fee) of "x" dollars, granting the sampler the use of the sample without owing any future mechanical royalties at all.

The whole area of "sampling" can frequently be a one-sided negotiation. Whether the publisher charges a high percentage, a low percentage or a small "buy-out" fee, the amount charged is up to the publisher of that pre-existing work since any use of the copyright without the permission of the copyright owner is, of course, an infringement.

I have had numerous situations where I or one of my co-publishers has determined that the new lyrics of a derivative work which sampled one of our copyrights was so offensive, we simply turned down the request altogether (or at least asked that the lyrics be rewritten). For those about to cry "censorship," I can only point out that one such request on my part for a lyric "cleanup" resulted in a gold single and a multi-platinum album. In its original form, the derivative work would have received no airplay at all!

To make the issue of sampling a little more complicated, let's say that a derivative work contains so much of the original work in question that the publisher of the pre-existing work determines that he wants to actually own or co-own the new work, rather than just share in the mechanical royalties and other income derived from the new work. This doesn't happen as often as you might assume. Why? Because those of us who receive a lot of sample requests have discovered that there frequently can be additional "uncleared" samples (i.e., samples for which the artist did not get permission) in the same song in which our pre-existing copyright is sampled. If the owner of the uncleared sample decides to sue for copyright infringement, my company gets sued too, because I am one of the owners of the new work in question.

Therefore, in the majority of situations that I'm familiar with, although the publisher of a pre-existing work continues to own that pre-existing work in its original form, that publisher will usually enter into an agreement with the "sampler" which grants the "pre-existing work" publisher an "income interest participation" in the new work, rather than actual copyright ownership of that work.

Are there exceptions? Sure there are. It's the music business! I've demanded copyright ownership on more than one occasion when so much of one of my songs was used that it would seem ridiculous not to require that I own the copyright in the derivative work. In most situations, however, I've taken the safest approach, which is to require an income interest participation in the mechanical royalties, as well as in the other types of royalties described in this chapter.

Finally, in an effort to be thorough, I should point out that the "sampler" not only has to get permission from the owner of the sampled copyright, but from the owner of the pre-existing master recording as well. To see just how costly sampling can become for a recording artist specializing in that medium, see the section on "controlled compositions" in chapter eight.

SYNCHRONIZATION ROYALTIES

Synchronization royalties are monies earned by publishers for granting the right to use a song in a film or television show. There isn't a compulsory synchronization rate. When it comes to determining how much to charge it's every publisher for him/herself.

Synchronization royalties are monies earned by publishers for granting the right to use a song in a film or television show. (Synchronization royalties are also earned on commercials and via "new media." See "Commercial Royalties," p. 57 and "New Media Royalties," p. 69.) The word synchronization refers to the fact that the song appears "in synch" with the visual images on the screen.

A synchronization license gives the film or television show the right to use the song. Unlike mechanical royalties, there isn't a compulsory synchronization rate. When it comes to determining how much to charge for the use of a song in a movie or TV show, it's every publisher for him/herself.

Negotiating "synch fees," as they are called in the business, is an art unto itself that can mean a difference of thousands of dollars to the publisher (and, of course,

MUSIC CLEARANCE ORGANIZATIONS

Music clearance organizations act as negotiators on behalf of parties wishing to use copyrighted music—mainly in the area of movies and television shows. Arlene Fishbach heads her own, extremely successful clearance organization, Arlene Fishbach Enterprises, based in Los Angeles. Arlene states the clearance organization's foremost activity: "Our primary function is to clear music—to act as an agent for the producer of a film or TV project—by negotiating synch fees and the rights acquired by payment of those fees so that nothing can stand in the way of the release of that project."

Arlene explains how this process typically works: "A producer will call us and say he's working on a project; he then tells us what it's all about: this includes a synopsis of the project, who's in it, where he's intending to distribute it once it's completed, and where he may plan on distributing it three or five years from now. Then we discuss what kind of music he wants.

"Sometimes he already has a specific idea of what songs he wants to use, sometimes he doesn't. Depending on how specific he is, we either recommend songs to him or we make preliminary plans to clear the songs he wants by discussing with him exactly what rights he needs.

"Usually what we will do is determine the best possible 'rights package' for him so that—in a year or eighteen months from now—if he decides he wants to distribute the product to the home video market, those rights will have already been negotiated for him. This way the publisher cannot say eighteen months later, 'OK, this is a real successful film; therefore, I want ten million dollars for my song to be used in the home video release.' Everything is negotiated up front in an effort to protect the producer and the distributor."

Why would a producer pay a music clearance agency to handle such negotiations rather than go directly to the specific publishers who control the songs he wants to use? Actually, some producers do go straight to the source.

For those who prefer to handle their own negotiations with publishers, clearance agencies can still perform a vital function. "For many clients all we do is research," Arlene says. "We'll supply them the publishing companies' names and the contacts who they can call themselves if they choose."

However, as Arlene points out, already having those personal contacts is a valuable asset for clearing houses. "This is a business that's based on relationships. A clearance organization that deals with the same publishers day in and day out usually can get faster and more thorough responses than an individual who doesn't know the major players in the publishing business."

to the songwriter whose publisher is doing the negotiating). In the case of motion pictures, payment for the use of a song in a film can be either very small for a low-budget film or up to hundreds of thousands of dollars for a big-budget film that uses a song as well as the song's title as the title of the movie.

Among the variables that can determine how much a publisher requests for a synch license are: the film's budget; the length of the use; whether the song is featured or is simply background music; the number of times the song is used in the film; whether the song is used over the opening or closing credits; and so on.

Once a publisher has been made aware that a film company wants to use one of his songs in a motion picture, the same strategy applies as in negotiating reduced mechanical rates: The film company wants to pay as little as possible, and the publisher wants to get as much as possible.

In many cases, film and television producers rely on music clearance organizations to handle the negotiation procedure for them. [See Music Clearance Organizations sidebar below.]

Unfortunately for the publisher, many film companies (or their appointed clearance organizations) begin the synch license negotiation process long before a film is completed (sometimes even before a film is started) so that the song can be dropped and substituted with another number from another publisher who is more willing to negotiate on the film company's terms.

Synchronization licenses differ from company to company. Usually the license will require that the royalty amount be paid within a certain amount of time (such as within thirty days; prior to the release of the film; or before the first airing of the TV show or commercial).

Real-life Scenario Number One

I was once contacted by a film company that wanted to use a song published by a firm I worked for. I was told that they might want to use the song both in the film and as the title, and that they wanted to negotiate a fee that would be higher than a "standard" use, but not nearly as high as I might usually charge for a title use, just in case they decided to go with another title.

One phone call to a friend of mine who had worked on the film got me all of the information I needed. The movie was already finished; the song in question was already the title of the film; the song was used over the closing credits; and the melody of the song appeared in the score throughout the picture. For the film company there was no turning back without spending several thousand dollars. Needless to say, I quoted a high fee and ignored the film company's complaints about my lack of fairness.

Was acquiring this inside information "cheating" on my part? Not really. After all, the film company was trying to mislead me by implying that a high fee could mean a loss of the song in the movie. The axiom that applies here is "All is fair in love, war and the music business."

Real-life Scenario Number Two

Synch fees for the use of a song in a documentary are generally much lower than those for feature films. The theory is that budgets for documentaries are usually quite low, as are the profits. This being the case, many music publishers grant synch licenses for documentaries for just a few thousand dollars—sometimes for just a few hundred dollars.

A few years ago I had just finished negotiating a $25,000 synch fee for the use of two songs in a documentary when I received a call requesting the use of two songs for $4,000 each in another documentary. I knew two things: that the budget for this second documentary was at least as large as the one I had just received twenty-five grand for, and that the second documentary would probably do extremely well at the box office since it was about a popular rock band. On top of everything else, one of the two songs was the same song I had just gotten $12,500 for in the first documentary.

Having done so well on documentary number one, I refused to grant synch licenses for the two songs in the second documentary for less than $10,000 each. To my surprise, the film company passed. The one thing I didn't take into account was that the second documentary wasn't finished yet.

Several months later the second documentary was released without the two songs from my publishing company in it. To make matters worse, along with the documentary was a soundtrack album that sold three million copies. If I had agreed to the original fee request of $8,000 for the two songs, and if both songs had appeared on the soundtrack album, I would have made much more in mechanical royalties than the $20,000 I was demanding for synch royalties in the first place.

At the time I made this blunder, the statutory mechanical rate was 5¼ cents. Two songs at 5¼ cents each times 3,000,000 comes to $315,000. Add the original synch license request of $8,000 for the two songs, and you'll see that I blew a possible gross of $323,000, all because I made the mistake of comparing one documentary deal with another, unrelated documentary deal. If you consider the fact that both songs could have been released as singles, the number goes even higher. All is fair. . . .

Commercial Royalties

There are several different types of synchronization licenses. Along with synch licenses for movies and television shows, there are also synch licenses for other specific types of uses, such as commercials, promotional videos, nontheatrical in-house meetings, pay/cable/subscription television (as opposed to "free" TV), and a variety of others.

In recent years, the amount of income that can be made from the use of a song in a commercial has increased substantially. The use of pop and Rock & Roll songs in advertising campaigns has become more and more commonplace because it is the music listened to by millions of American consumers.

In recent years, the amount of income that can be made from the use of a song in a commercial has increased substantially.

Some publishers have commanded (and gotten) more than a million dollars for the use of a current hit or Rock & Roll "standard" to advertise beer, soft drinks, credit cards, computers and other items. This is obviously the extremely high end of the synch fee spectrum but it has happened on several occasions.

In most cases, publishers are contacted by advertising agencies representing a particular product. Usually the agency asks for a one-year license with an option to use the song for additional years if the campaign is successful.

As is the case with motion pictures, the amount of money a publisher can get for such a use depends primarily on the budget for the commercial. The bigger the budget, the higher the synch fee is going to be.

There is usually a lot of guesswork involved in negotiations of this type. No doubt, many publishers have asked for a fee much lower than the advertising agency might have been willing to pay.

Some parameters that publishers use to consider what fee to ask for are: 1) the territory involved; 2) the duration (or term) of the license; 3) the length of the commercial; 4) the importance of the song being licensed; 5) whether or not the commercial will be used on radio as well as television; 6) whether or not there will be a "parody" lyric involved; and 7) whether or not the advertiser requests an exclusive use. Let's consider these factors individually:

A publisher will be inclined to ask more for a commercial that is longer, such as sixty seconds, than for one that is thirty seconds long.

1. Commercial Territory. Some commercials are "national," some are "local," while others fall into some sort of middle ground. A commercial advertising a product such as laundry detergent is usually of the national variety. In other words, it appears all over the country during a commercial break of a network show.

   A commercial advertising a small clothing store in your neighborhood is a local commercial that is seen only in your viewing area.

   Commercials that can fall somewhere in between a national and a local advertisement are those that appear only in specific regions. If an auto parts store has branches only in St. Louis, Chicago and Miami, then those are the only regions where the commercial will air.

   There are also commercials known as spot advertisements in which the product may be of a national nature, but the commercial is shown in specific regions at different times.

   Therefore, the territory of a commercial can demand any number of variations regarding the fee that might be asked by the publisher.

   A national commercial will bring thousands of dollars more than a local commercial, whereas commercials that are shown in only three or four major cities will usually fall somewhere in between.

2. Commercial Term. The duration of a commercial use can be anywhere from very brief (sometimes only a day or a week) to interminable. Once again, the synch fee involved can be very small for a short campaign or well over a million dollars for a multiyear use.

   If an ad agency requests the use of a song for a year with an option to use it for a second year, it is a common practice among publishers to grant the option request, provided that the advertiser agrees to pay a synch fee that is anywhere from 10 to 20 percent higher for the second year.

   In other words, if a dog food company wants to use "I Love My Dog" for one year with a one-year option, the publisher of "I Love My Dog" might agree to a fee of $100,000 for one year, with a 15 percent increase for the second year. If the commercial causes the dog food company to sell a lot of dog food, they will probably want to use the song for a second year.

   Under the license agreement the dog food company has with the publisher, upon picking up the option for the second year, the dog food company will owe the publisher $115,000 (or $100,000 plus 15 percent of $100,000). So, for the two years combined, the publisher has grossed $215,000. Of course, since the second year is an "option," if the dog food company decides not to use the song after the end of the first year, no more synch royalties are due to the publisher.

The variations on the commercial term are numerous. I have been involved with one song that was used to advertise a particular product for nine years. I'm sure there are others that have gone on even longer.

3. Commercial Length. The length of commercials varies from as short as ten seconds to as long as a minute and a half. In special situations (such as when a national soft drink is introducing a superstar as a new spokesperson), the length of a commercial can be even longer.

   Just as negotiating a movie synch fee, a publisher will be inclined to ask more for a commercial that is longer, such as sixty seconds, than for one that is thirty seconds long.

4. Importance of Song. This is a factor that can make a difference of thousands of dollars in the publisher's asking price. Although it should be obvious, the importance of a song can sometimes be overlooked, especially by a major publisher dealing with thousands of copyrights.

   Determining the importance of a song is, in some ways, subjective. However, it should be obvious that a song that has become a "standard" via multiple recordings and continued popularity over a long period of time is more important than a song that was once a minor hit.

   There is also the question of the importance of the song to the advertiser. If a particular song is obviously the perfect choice for a product, a publisher will probably be able to charge more to that advertiser than to another who simply happened to like the song's melody.

   Some publishers have songs that they consider to be of too much historical and/or social importance to allow any advertiser to use. Others consider a song "too important" until someone offers an amount of money large enough to change their minds.

   Some publishers have songs that they consider to be of too much historical and/or social importance to allow any advertiser to use.

   Many songwriters have clauses in their publishing agreements that allow the writer the final decision about whether or not his song will be used to advertise a product or service, as well as the manner in which the song will be used.

5. Commercials on Radio. To refer to a radio commercial use as a "synch" use is actually a misnomer, since there are no images to synchronize the music with. However, since many advertisers sometimes use the same audio track for a radio commercial as for a TV commercial, the term "synch license" or commercial synch license is usually used even to denote a license for a commercial used only on radio.

   If an advertiser wants to use a song in both TV and radio commercials, the publisher will almost always ask more than he would ask for a commercial used just on television.

   Under similar circumstances, advertisers usually expect to pay less for a song used only on a radio commercial than for the same song used only on a TV commercial.

6. Parody Lyrics. Here's another word publishers sometimes use improperly. The word parody actually means a humorous or farcical recasting of a literary or musical work. In the music publishing business, a parody lyric can also mean

Many songwriters have clauses in their publishing agreements that allow the writer the final decision about whether or not his song will be used to advertise a product or service, as well as the manner in which the song will be used.

RANDY'S THOUGHTS ON THE USE OF ROCK & ROLL HITS IN COMMERCIALS

There have been loud complaints by some prominent rock stars in the last few years regarding the use of Rock & Roll hits in commercials. Their arguments are usually based on the fact that these songs are of historical significance; that they are pieces of art being wrongfully used to sell soap, soft drinks and other products; or that, by allowing a song to be used in such a manner, the song's creator is "selling out" (that's a term we used to use in the 1960s).

In many ways I can see their point. How can a particular superstar possibly need any more money? Does he really have to turn one of his biggest hits into a sixty-second commercial for Pepsi or Coke? Surely the only reason he could possibly do such a thing is because he's being paid in the millions of dollars. It can't be solely because he "believes in the product." Otherwise, why wouldn't he just make the commercial for free?

I used to have the same attitude: No Rock & Roll standard should be used in a commercial. However, I've since learned that many of those songs were written by songwriters who aren't superstars. A few years ago I was involved in licensing a song that you have probably heard hundreds of times. Before I made the commercial deals, the song had been earning the writer a few hundred dollars a year in performance income because it still got a lot of airplay on radio stations that played "oldies."

In a matter of months I issued two commercial synch licenses for the song that totalled over $100,000. It was the most money that songwriter had ever seen, and he was extremely grateful. Of course I won't embarrass him by mentioning his name, but he was over seventy years old when I made the deals. His share was enough for him to retire on. He even spent some of it to go into the studio and make more demos!

So, I have—to some extent—changed my mind about the use of Rock & Roll songs in commercials. The superstars who turn their hits into jingles may be suffering from some serious greed, but that elderly gentleman who wrote the song I'm referring to finally made the kind of money he would have made a long time ago if the mechanical royalty rate had been higher— and if other sources of income (such as the use of Rock & Roll songs in commercials) had been available to him then.

that the lyrics of a song have been changed to advertise a product. All of us have heard commercials on television in which the melody of a familiar song has been used in conjunction with lyrics that promote a particular product.

When a copyrighted song is used in a commercial, performance royalties are paid by the performance rights society with which the song's publisher and song-writer are affiliated. Some performing rights societies pay less for the performance of a parody lyric used in a commercial than if the original lyrics are used. (Don't ask me why. It's just one of the mysteries of the music business.) Therefore, some publishers will charge more for the use of a song if the advertiser insists on changing the lyrics since the ensuing performing royalty income will be less.

Once again, in many cases a songwriter's contract with a publisher will include a clause that gives the songwriter the final say in any lyric changes of this type.

7. Exclusive Use. In the advertising business there are several types of exclusive uses. The most common is referred to as "exclusive to product." For instance, if the dog food company mentioned earlier wants to use "I Love My Dog," they will ask that they have the exclusive use of the song for pet food commercials for the duration of the commercial term.

If the ASPCA wants to use the same song to advertise the importance of being kind to animals, the publisher can allow that use since it doesn't conflict with the dog food company's use.

Another type of exclusive refers to a particular territory. If the dog food company advertises and sells its dog food only in California, it might ask for product exclusivity for the state of California. The publisher can then allow another dog food company that advertises and sells its product only in New York to use the same song. However, the publisher has to be cautious in granting product exclusivity for just one state or a small group of states. If a national dog food company wants to use "I Love My Dog" for a commercial that would cover the entire U.S., and the publisher has already granted an "exclusive to product" license for "I Love My Dog" to a dog food company in California, then the national dog food company is going to start looking for another song. It's up to the publisher to decide whether the use in California is worth the gamble of possibly blowing a national use.

Sometimes the situation can be even more complicated, because there are occasions when an advertiser will ask for *total* exclusivity on a song. In this case, the publisher will usually ask for more money than he would in almost any other synch license situation. The reason the publisher can be expected to charge a large fee is because the advertiser is asking the publisher to give up the chance to allow any other advertisers of any type of product to use that particular song for the duration of the commercial term.

Granting total exclusivity on a song is almost always a roll of the dice for the publisher. Some songs just seem to lend themselves to commercials. There are several songs in one of the publishing companies I have managed about which we received calls almost every week. If I had decided to grant a total exclusive on one of those songs, I would have been passing up the opportunity to allow the same song to be used in other ad campaigns. Therefore, if an ad agency requests an exclusive license on a song, the publishing company's licensing department has to ask for an amount equal to or higher than the amount it estimates the song would have received if several "exclusive to product" uses had been granted.

PERFORMANCE ROYALTIES

As I said in chapter two, one of the five exclusive rights of the copyright owner is "the right to perform (or authorize others to perform) the copyrighted work publicly."

Beginning with ASCAP in 1914, and later with BMI and SESAC, there are three performing rights societies in the United States that make sure the copyright owners of songs are paid performance royalties when those songs are performed in public.

The three societies issue licenses to those companies and establishments that publicly perform (or allow others to publicly perform) music as a part of their business operation. The licenses issued require these music users to make payments to the performing rights societies for the right to perform the songs that belong in the societies' repetoires. Specifically, such users of music include radio and television stations, restaurants, nightclubs, dance halls, and other venues and broadcasters.

Once the societies determine the amount of performance royalties owed to the music publishers and songwriters of those songs being performed, the societies make payments to the appropriate parties. For example, a performance of a song on a television show would lead to performance royalties being paid to the publisher and songwriter of that particular song by the performing rights society with which that publisher and writer are affiliated.

The societies do the legwork required to make sure both songwriters and music publishers are properly compensated for public performances.

The societies do the legwork required to make sure both songwriters and music publishers are properly compensated for public performances, since it would be impossible for the individual writers and publishers to keep track of every time their songs are performed.

Of course, it's also impossible for the societies to keep track of *every* performance, so each society has devised its own system to come as close as possible to making accurate assessments of performances and then to make payments to writers and publishers based on the methods that each society has developed.

Before we begin to explore the three performing rights societies individually, there are several important pieces of information you should know, beginning with the relationship between the songwriter, the publisher and the societies.

A writer can belong to only one society at a time, although two or more writers of the same song can belong to two or more societies. In other words, Al can be a member of ASCAP, Bob can be affiliated with BMI, and Sally can belong to SESAC. If the three of them write a song together, each will be paid his or her share of performance royalties by the performing rights society to which he or she belongs.

The same is true for publishers. Al's publishing company "A" must be a member of ASCAP; Bob's publisher "B" must be with BMI; and Sally's publishing company "S" must be affiliated with SESAC. Many publishing firms actually consist of several different publishing companies, each affiliated with one of the three societies.

Although a publishing company rarely changes its affiliation from one society to another (primarily because it would mean all of the writers signed to that publisher would have to be able and willing to change their affiliations simultaneously), many songwriters have been known to switch societies at some time in their careers. However, no songwriter or single publishing company can be affiliated with more than one society at a time.

It is also very important to note that the three U.S. performing rights societies license something called small rights, or nondramatic performances, that is, performances of songs on radio, television, in nightclubs, hotels, and so forth. Grand rights, which include the rights granted to perform songs in a Broadway show or any other dramatic context, are outside the realm of the performing rights societies. [See "Royalties for Grand Rights," p. 66.]

ASCAP

ASCAP stands for the American Society of Composers, Authors and Publishers. (The term "authors" as used in this context is synonymous with the word "lyricists.") ASCAP was founded in New York City in 1914, making it the first performing rights society in the country.

ASCAP was created so that those performing music publicly would finally be forced to comply with the Copyright Act, which had added public performance to the list of the copyright owner's exclusive rights a few years earlier, and of course, to pay the copyright owners royalties for those public performances.

ASCAP acquires monies to pay copyright owners by licensing (issuing a license and charging a fee to) "users" of music for public performance. Among the licensees who pay fees to ASCAP are: the major television networks, local and cable television, radio stations, public broadcasters, colleges and universities, restaurants, hotels, concert halls, Muzak and other users.

Among the licensees who pay fees to ASCAP are: the major television networks, radio stations, restaurants, hotels, concert halls, Muzak and other users.

The licensing fees ASCAP charges to users vary depending on the size of the licensee and the amount of music generally used. A local television station will be charged a much lower fee than a network, while a small restaurant will pay less than a radio station in a major market.

How much is to be charged for a license to use songs in the ASCAP repertory is determined, in some cases, by negotiations such as those between ASCAP and organizations like the American Hotel and Motel Association. If a user feels the fee is too high, that user can ask a New York federal judge to determine a reasonable fee.

There are certain situations where a user of music doesn't use ASCAP songs (such as a restaurant that plays only classical music in the public domain), in which case ASCAP cannot issue a license. Other users may have ASCAP songs performed so seldomly that they may opt to negotiate a performance fee directly with the copyright owners of the specific work being performed. The concept of direct licensing has always been an option available to users. However, those who frequently have ASCAP songs being performed will almost always agree to pay the fee for ASCAP's "blanket license," giving the user the right to use any song that is in ASCAP's repertoire.

As I said earlier, each of the performing rights societies has devised systems for tracking performances. ASCAP uses tapes of actual radio broadcasts, as well as logs from radio stations, to determine which writers and publishers are due monies from radio performances. Thousands of hours of radio broadcasts around the country are surveyed each year.

Television royalties are paid out on the basis of a census, or complete count, of all performances on network TV (ABC, CBS and NBC, as well as the Fox, Paramount and Warner Bros. networks). In addition, ASCAP surveys more than two million hours of local television broadcasts annually, covering a virtual census of syndicated series, feature films and movies of the week.

Marilyn Bergman, ASCAP president and chairman since 1994, explains some of the reasons she's an ASCAP advocate: "ASCAP is a remarkable organization. It is, in fact, the premiere performing rights organization in the world. It is the most fair, the most dependable and the most protective of creators' rights. We pay royalties based on earnings and based on fairness. The most successful and the newest guy on the block get paid the same amount for comparable performance.

And you can rely on ASCAP throughout your career—not just at a particular high point, but as a steady, solid support.

"We are the only United States society that is owned by writers and publishers, and whose president is a writer. This structure uniquely equips us to best understand the needs of our 72,000 active composers, lyricists and publisher members, unencumbered by any other interests.

"ASCAP is also the only United States society that conducts open membership meetings and issues complete financial reports to its members.

"We were the first to offer our members important benefits such as a credit union and instrument insurance; the first to establish an innovative system called ACE (the ASCAP Clearance Express) to make title, writer and publisher information available through ASCAP's World Wide Website.

"ASCAP is also the acknowledged leader in revenue collections and royalty distributions, and in negotiating license fees with the users of music. ASCAP is committed to ensuring that our members receive the highest payment possible when their music is performed outside the United States. To that end, ASCAP has instituted 'technical visits' to foreign societies to ensure proper identification and crediting of our members' performed works, and we have also welcomed their visits to ASCAP to learn more about our operations firsthand.

"Since 1914, ASCAP has aggressively championed creators' rights and continues to assume leadership in this area as our music enters cyberspace. In fact, we have a 'new media' license which is considered a model license in the digital world.

"And while we are busy making sure our members are getting paid for getting played, we continue to build new careers and catalogs via the workshops, showcases and educational programs sponsored by the ASCAP Foundation.

"These are the reasons I am a member of ASCAP—and why I choose to remain a member. In all ways I can think of, it pays to belong to ASCAP."

BMI

Broadcast Music, Inc.—BMI—was formed in 1940, providing ASCAP with its first serious competition. Prior to the founding of BMI, songwriters and publishers of some types of music had been denied the right to share in performance royalty income. BMI president Frances Preston explains: "In 1940 BMI initiated 'the Open Door Policy' extending participation in performing rights income to all creators of all types of music at a time when they were denied participation by other American performing rights societies. This policy helped facilitate the great explosion of American Music that has continued throughout the history of BMI."

Whatever its reasons, ASCAP had chosen to deny membership to writers and publishers of rhythm and blues and country, as well as some other types of music. (To be fair, I should mention that today all three U.S. performing rights societies are open to all types of music.)

In the late 1930s, realizing the niche that was available to them at the time, approximately six hundred broadcasting enterprises decided to form BMI. These broadcasters felt that the fees they were being charged by ASCAP were too high. During 1940, BMI affiliated many publishers and songwriters. ASCAP's contract with the broadcasters expired on December 31 of that year, and suddenly there were no ASCAP songs being broadcast. By airing only non-ASCAP songs on the radio, the broadcasters were attempting to avoid paying the fees ASCAP was demanding. Meanwhile, the Justice Department filed civil suits alleging antitrust violations on the parts of ASCAP, BMI, NBC and CBS.

Both BMI and ASCAP eventually signed consent decrees to settle their suits. ASCAP resolved its negotiations with the broadcasters, and soon the music of both societies was back on the airwaves.

Like ASCAP, BMI issues licenses to those who are involved in the public performance of music. BMI licenses television and radio stations, cable program services, radio and TV networks, PBS, restaurants, nightclubs and many other users of music.

Like ASCAP, BMI issues licenses to those who are involved in the public performance of music.

BMI's method of tracking performances is through a scientific sampling. For radio, BMI requires various stations to keep logs of music they broadcast during a specific time period. Different stations are asked to keep logs at different times of the year. These logs are then analyzed by BMI's computer system, which scientifically determines the probable number of times the songs were performed by all similarly formatted radio stations during that quarter. For television, BMI uses a national database similar to the type used by *TV Guide* for keeping track of the listings of songs being performed on syndicated programs, and relies on cue sheets provided by the networks and cable suppliers to calculate the performances of BMI-licensed music in those media.

BMI pays its writers and publishers from all of the licensing fees collected throughout the country after deducting its overhead and fees to be paid to foreign societies.

Frances Preston gives some of the reasons she considers BMI the best society for writers and publishers: "BMI is responsible for most innovations in the performing rights field including being the first to distribute royalties for FM radio airplay and television background music, and now, the first to create a distinct and complete logging and distribution system for college radio airplay.

"We have always led the way in creating awards and recognition through the media for our songwriters and composers. We are proud of all the musical genres in our repertoire and all the creators of music who have entrusted us with their representation. These include Michael Jackson, Gloria Estefan, Willie Nelson, Paul Simon, John Williams and 65,000 others.

"BMI has always led the way in the fight to protect the rights of composers, songwriters and copyright owners locally, nationally and internationally. We also employ the most advanced technological systems of any performing rights organization in the world. Our staff prides itself on the quality of service we provide to the largest and most creative body of composers, songwriters and publishers anywhere in the world."

SESAC

Of the three performing rights societies, SESAC runs a distant third in size. The organization was formed by Paul Heinecke in 1930, at which time it was called the Society of European Stage Authors and Composers. In earlier days SESAC primarily represented European works. Since this is no longer its main function, the society has reduced its name to simply SESAC.

Although there are similarities between the functions of SESAC and the other two U.S. performing rights societies, SESAC is profoundly different because it is a privately owned company. In fact, SESAC was purchased most recently, in 1992,

Although there are similarities between the functions of SESAC and the other two U.S. performing rights societies, SESAC is profoundly different because it is a privately owned company.

by Freddie Gershon, Ira Smith and Stephen Swid (remember him from SBK in chapter one?) along with the merchant banking house of Allen & Company.

Whereas BMI and ASCAP operate on a not-for-profit basis and pay most of the money they collect to songwriters and publishers, SESAC pays out approximately half of its earnings to its affiliates, keeping the rest for company profits. However, according to SESAC's president and COO, William Velez, "By virtue of applying a selective policy as to the acquisition of repertory, SESAC can afford to maintain more than competitive payment to our writers and publishing."

Also, SESAC actively works with its members in the areas of catalog consulting, legal advice, teaming up songwriters for collaboration purposes, and other personalized functions.

Another area in which SESAC is unique among the societies is in its manner of determining performances. Velez states, "While the traditional television cue sheet still serves as the basis for SESAC's television payments, the organization has distinguished itself by employing state-of-the-art digital pattern recognition technology for the purpose of tracking radio performances in virtually all genres. This technology, patented by a firm named Broadcast Data Systems, is currently used as the source for *Billboard*'s industry trade charts and gives SESAC the capability of tracking 8.3 million hours of radio programming annually, versus about 800,000 hours for ASCAP and BMI combined.

"SESAC also pays faster, because the organization distributes royalties within one quarter of the actual performance quarter, as opposed to a two to three quarters lag time at ASCAP and BMI."

Like the other two societies, SESAC issues licenses to users of music for public performance and has reciprocal arrangements with foreign societies. Velez also points out that SESAC is opening new doors in the area of foreign societies: "SESAC is the first U.S. performing rights organization to establish relations with China having executed a reciprocal agreement in May of 1996."

Royalties for Grand Rights

Grand rights—also known as "dramatic performance rights"—are the rights granted to publicly perform musical compositions in a dramatic setting (plays, ballets, Broadway shows, and so on). As you have already learned, the three performing rights societies are generally limited to licensing "small rights," or "nondramatic rights," and wouldn't be involved in negotiating grand rights.

A theater group that is planning to perform a musical on Broadway would have to negotiate and pay dramatic performance rights royalties to the copyright owner of the compositions in that musical. Because dramatic performance rights are so uniquely different from some of the other types of rights we have covered, the rules governing their administration sometimes differ as well.

Often, songwriters who write specifically for the theater reserve to themselves the right to license grand rights. In some cases, writers who don't compose for the theater also reserve the right to license grand rights just in case one of their songs is chosen to be included in a musical or other dramatic setting. Therefore, although the publisher of a musical might control other types of rights in the individual songs from that musical (granting synch rights, issuing mechanical licenses, negotiating print deals, etc.), granting grand rights will be controlled by the writers of that musical.

The Imaginary Musical Scenario

Roger Dietz and Murray Heart have written a musical entitled *Paint Your Trailer.* For the sake of this scenario let's say that Dietz and Heart are signed to Sam's Bigtime Publishing Company, but that the copyright ownership of the dramatic rights are in the names of Dietz and Heart. Therefore, if the Raving Lunatics Repertory Company wishes to put on a production of *Paint Your Trailer* at a particular venue, they must negotiate the grand rights royalty fees with the copyright owners— in this case, Dietz and Heart.

Dietz and Heart have granted Sam's publishing company the right to negotiate and issue licenses for other types of royalties (synch licenses, for instance). One of the twelve songs in *Paint Your Trailer* is called "Sodas, Sodas, Sodas." When a major soft drink company decided that "Sodas, Sodas, Sodas" would be the perfect song to use in their next ad campaign, the commercial synch license had to be negotiated with (and issued by) Sam's Bigtime Publishing Company.

The royalties from the Raving Lunatics Repertory Company were paid directly to Dietz and Heart. On the other hand, the synch royalties for the soft drink commercial were paid to Sam's Bigtime Publishing Company, which in turn paid Dietz and Heart their respective songwriter's shares when the songwriters' next royalty statements were due.

Now let's say that Dietz and Heart are affiliated with BMI. We already know that, in this case, grand rights are the domain of the two writers. However, the musical is a big success, and another song from the show—"They Call the Breeze Belinda"—becomes a hit record by William Andies. The mechanical license would be issued to Mr. Andies's record company by either Sam's Bigtime Publishing Company or the Harry Fox Agency. When Sam receives mechanical royalties, he would keep his share and pay the writers their shares. And when the recording of "They Call the Breeze Belinda" is played on the radio, or the song is performed by William on a late night talk show, those performances fall into the category of nondramatic rights. BMI would then pay Sam's publishing company for the publisher's share of small performance rights royalties, and Dietz and Heart would each be paid by BMI for their songwriters' shares of small performance rights royalties.

The Grand Rights Exception

Not every musical that appears on the stage is made up of a group of songs written by a writer specifically for that musical. There have been several theatrical shows that have consisted of songs written by various songwriters during a particular era. A musical about the early days of Rock & Roll, for instance, might consist of fifteen or twenty different Rock & Roll hits of the late 1950s. Obviously, in 1955 those songwriters had no way of knowing that their songs would eventually become a part of a popular musical thirty years later. Therefore, it is not likely that there would have been provisions for excluding grand rights from the rights acquired by the various publishers of those songs. Also, the publishers would have had no reason to consider granting such rights, since the songs weren't written specifically for a musical in the first place (as the aforementioned Dietz and Heart songs obviously were). In this case, the publisher (as opposed to the songwriters) would be in a position to grant grand rights to the party wishing to put on the musical in question. Grand rights royalties would then be paid to the publishers, who would each pay their writers the individual songwriters' shares.

The Real-Life Musical Scenario

When I wrote the first edition of this book, there were no plans in the works for what is now affectionately referred to around my office as "the smash hit Broadway musical *Smokey Joe's Cafe: The Songs of Leiber & Stoller*." As it turns out *Smokey Joe's* just happens to fall into the category described above. That is, the show consists of almost forty songs written by Jerry Leiber and Mike Stoller over the course of several decades, beginning back in 1952.

Luckily, in this particular case, the songwriters happen to own the publishing on most of the songs that appear in the show. However, the rights to those songs owned by outside publishers had to be negotiated between those outside publishers and the company that produced the musical. Furthermore, there were some songs used in *Smokey Joe's* for which a few subpublishers (see chapter five for an explanation of "subpublishing") had the rights in their particular territories. Therefore, before the show could be performed overseas, the producers had to negotiate with those subpublishers to have the right to perform some of the show's songs in the particular territories those subpublishers control.

Having now gone through this process, I would strongly recommend that young songwriters do their best to specifically exclude grand rights from their songwriter agreements. *Smokey Joe's Cafe: The Songs of Leiber & Stoller* is solid evidence that you never know when your songs might be used in the context of a theatrical production.

PRINT ROYALTIES

Print royalties are monies earned from the sale of printed editions of songs. As I said in chapter one, this was the original source of income for music publishers and songwriters when music publishing was in its infancy in this country. Although print royalties have generally taken a back seat to mechanical, synchronization and performance income, the printed editions of songs are still an important part of music publishing today.

Print royalties differ from other types of publishing income, since printed music is not handled by all publishing companies in the same manner. For instance, some music publishers are large enough that they still print sheet music, folios, orchestral arrangements and other printed editions with their own facilities. Other publishers rely on companies known as print publishers to print music for them. Since so few music publishers are still in the market of printing their own sheet music and other printed editions, let's turn our attention to the print publisher.

Print publishers are a very competitive breed. Their survival usually depends on acquiring the rights to create printed editions of hit songs. Because of this, print publishers attempt to make exclusive deals with copyright-owning publishers. These exclusive deals give the print publisher the right to create printed editions of all of the songs in the copyright-owning publisher's catalog for a particular length of time. One print publisher can own the print rights of a large number of copyright-owning publishers at one time.

The print publisher usually pays an advance to the copyright-owning publisher, followed by a percentage of royalties the print publisher earns from sales of the printed editions.

The rights the print publisher acquires (depending on the parameters of the agreement) can include the rights to print sheet music, folios, and arrangements for choruses, bands and orchestras. In exchange for these rights, the print publisher usually pays an advance to the copyright-owning publisher, followed by a percentage of royalties the print publisher earns from sales of the printed editions.

Of these various printed editions, sheet music is probably the most frequently published. Surprisingly, however, not all hit songs are considered marketable as sheet music. Due to the high costs of printing, print publishers tend to print only those songs that either make it to the very top of the charts or that become standards over a period of time. Unlike the majority of the record-buying public, sheet music purchasers are usually musicians who want to learn how to play the song in question. Although a dance record with two chords and one lyrical phrase repeated over and over may become a big hit on the radio and among record buyers, sheet music sales would probably be minimal. A simple dance tune might come and go without ever being printed as sheet music.

A visit to the sheet music section of your local music store can be a very enlightening experience. What you will usually find in the racks are several current hits and dozens of standards from all eras. These standards will usually include pop ballads, gospel songs, songs frequently used at weddings and the songs you hear performed by lounge acts around the globe.

Another type of printed edition is the folio. Folios are better known as songbooks to you and me. These folios come in a variety of styles including mixed, matching and personality.

A mixed folio consists of a grab bag of songs that have something in common. Rock & Roll hits from the 1950s, favorite movie themes, and classic country songs would all be examples of mixed folios.

Many times a print publisher will release a folio that contains all of the songs from a hit album. Often this matching folio will have the same cover as the album in question. Another example of a matching folio would be one that comprises all of the songs used in a popular movie.

Personality folios differ from matching folios, since the personality may be a nonperforming songwriter or songwriting team, or the folio may contain hits from various albums by the same artist.

Those of us who have played in the school marching band or have sung in a choir are familiar with the many different types of arrangements available in printed editions. There are also folios and sheet music for easy piano, organ, guitar and all other popular instruments.

NEW MEDIA ROYALTIES

Once again, the music publishing community makes up a name that doesn't necessarily mean what it's called. "New media" is a sort of catch-all phrase for the newer technologies that have come into existence over the last few years. Karaoke and MIDI (musical instrument digital interface) are two technologies that used to be part of the category known as "new media." Now that people in the publishing business know what they are and how to deal with them, we call them Karaoke and MIDI just like everybody else does. Other "new media" are such things as DVD (Digital Videodisc), CD-ROM (compact disc-read-only memory), CD+G (compact disc plus graphics), CD-i (compact disc-interactive), other forms of enhanced CDs and the Internet. The technology is coming fast and furiously, and music publishers (as well as other copyright owners) are desperately trying to keep up with it all.

Not all hit songs are considered marketable as sheet music.

Determining how to negotiate rates for these new areas is a constant concern for the copyright owners. In some cases, specific types of "new media" are comprised of most of the other royalty areas discussed in this chapter. For instance, if a device includes a recording of a song, then mechanical royalties come into play. That same device might also have moving images, in which case a synchronization with the music has taken place. If that same "new media" allows lyrics to be seen or printed, then print income is due. If your publishing company has a deal with a "print publisher," then the print publisher might demand, in some cases, to have the right to collect the print income, while your publisher would claim to have the right to collect mechanical and synch income. If the music can be manipulated and changed, then one can create derivative works of the original copyright—but let's not even get into that!

Most publishers have found ways to deal with all of the "new media" that now exists. Others are hanging on by the seat of their pants. The important thing to keep in mind is that all of these new technologies mean new sources of income for the music publisher and the songwriter.

SUMMARY

All of the types of royalties we have covered are available to songwriters and music publishers because of the U.S. Copyright Act. The five exclusive rights discussed in chapter two provide the copyright owner the right, by law, to receive mechanical, synchronization, performance, print and "new media" royalties. In the next chapter you will see that there is protection for songs in most territories outside of the United States as well, thanks to international copyright laws.

Five

ROYALTIES FROM FOREIGN SOURCES

*I*t has been said that the popular songs created in this country are America's greatest ambassadors to the rest of the world. Since American music is listened to around the globe, royalties are generally being earned wherever that music is played.

Not wanting to miss out on opportunities to earn income from a song's use, publishers have devised methods by which they can be compensated for their works gathering royalties on foreign soil, just as foreign copyright owners receive royalties when their songs are recorded and performed in the United States.

Of course, our government helped pave the way by having the United States become a member of the Universal Copyright Convention and—more recently—the Berne Convention. These multinational conventions cause many countries to recognize copyrights created in the United States as having the same protection as their own domestic copyrights.

There are some countries that don't belong to either of the conventions mentioned above. Some of these nonmember nations have direct treaties with the United States; some countries' copyright relationships with the United States are officially listed as "unclear" by the Copyright Office; and a few countries have no copyright agreements with the United States at all.

Going through detailed explanations of which countries recognize U.S. copyrights under which specific treaties would be a lengthy and boring exercise. Germany, Spain, the United Kingdom, France, Japan, Belgium, Holland, Italy, Australia, Mexico, Argentina and Brazil all recognize U.S. copyrights. Countries such as Iran, Iraq, Oman and Qatar don't. At this point in history it's a safe assumption that there aren't too many American pop songs being played in Iran, so U.S. publishers probably aren't missing out on large sums of royalties there.

The main method of acquiring royalties from countries that do recognize U.S. copyrights is through a process called "subpublishing." For example, if my publishing company owns a copyright that becomes a hit in England, I need to have an agreement with a British publishing company so it can collect royalties earned on the song in the United Kingdom. Based on the conditions provided by my company's agreement with the British firm, that company (known as the subpublisher) will pay my publishing company a percentage of all of the monies

Publishers have devised methods by which they can be compensated for their works gathering royalties on foreign soil, just as foreign copyright owners receive royalties when their songs are recorded and performed in the United States.

it collects that are earned by the song originally published by my company in the United States.

The concept of subpublishing is actually rather simple. It tends to become confusing because there are a variety of different routes a U.S. publishing company can take to have proper foreign representation. On top of that, subpublishing agreements can vary widely. Add to this the difficulty of dealing with a language barrier, foreign currencies and "partners" who are thousands of miles away, and you can begin to see how the simple concept of subpublishing can become extremely complicated.

TWO MAIN AVENUES OF FOREIGN REPRESENTATION

When a song is a hit in the United States, there is frequently foreign activity on the work as well. The U.S. publisher has two main choices for foreign representation, either: 1) country-by-country subpublishing agreements or 2) a single, worldwide subpublishing agreement.

When a song is a hit in the United States, there is frequently foreign activity on the work as well. If a hit song belongs to a new publishing company in the United States, the new publisher will need to determine how he wishes to have his company represented in other countries. The U.S. publisher has two main choices for foreign representation, either: 1) country-by-country subpublishing agreements or 2) a single, worldwide subpublishing agreement with a multinational subpublisher—a company that already has subpublishing agreements in place or owns its own subpublishing companies around the world.

There are advantages and disadvantages to both choices. First let's consider the advantages of country-by-country subpublishing agreements. If a song originating in the United States becomes a hit in England, the U.S. publisher can negotiate an agreement with a British subpublisher whereby the British company will agree to pay a large advance to the American publisher. If the song becomes a hit in Germany a few weeks later, the U.S. publisher can then enter into a subpublishing agreement with a German publisher, acquiring another advance from the German publisher for the right to represent the song in his territory. As the song becomes a hit around the world, the U.S. publisher can continue to negotiate deals with publishers in each new country the song reaches, collecting advances from the individual subpublishers until the song has achieved worldwide representation.

Since there will probably be several companies in each country vying for sub-publishing rights to the song, the U.S. publisher will usually have the upper hand in the negotiating procedures. In the end, he will come away with advances from each country and—if he has a good entertainment lawyer—the best possible deal from each of the subpublishers.

On the other hand, the U.S. publisher will now have over a dozen subpublishing agreements to keep track of, complicated by the fact that each agreement may have different terms and different percentages to be collected. Also, if there is a dispute about payments due from, say, Scandinavia, a lawsuit would probably prove to be impractical.

The U.S. publisher's other choice for representation would be a single administration agreement with a large, multinational publishing company that already has representation outside of the United States. If a song becomes a hit abroad, the song's U.S. publisher would need to sign only one agreement that would cover the entire world. If a problem arose in a particular foreign country, the U.S. publisher could require the administrating publisher to resolve the problem. Also, the single subpublishing administration agreement is usually uniform for all of the countries involved, rather than the group of assorted contracts possible in a country-by-country situation.

The major disadvantage of a single administration agreement is that there would be only one advance for the entire world, which would—in all likelihood—be substantially less than the total of all advances the song's U.S. publisher could have acquired on a country-by-country basis. Then there is the matter of how much attention the U.S. publisher's song will receive. After all, the administrating publisher has a catalog of its own songs to worry about—songs that may be making far more money for them than they will earn from simply representing your song in foreign countries for a small percentage.

Of course, the fact that the U.S. publisher might be receiving less money doesn't negate the fact that having several subpublishers is also a very costly exercise. Therefore, the U.S. publisher might end up with essentially the same amount of money in either situation after the song's success has run its course.

A THIRD AVENUE OF FOREIGN REPRESENTATION

The U.S. publisher has a third option for collecting foreign royalties due, although it is not a common route chosen by many publishers. A U.S. publisher affiliated with the Harry Fox Agency may request that Fox collect foreign royalties via HFA's agreements with foreign collection societies and agencies. The advantage to using Fox is that there is no percentage to give up to a subpublisher. However, there are several disadvantages, including that there are no advances offered, no exploitation of the publisher's songs, and no attempts to acquire foreign language recordings. Most U.S. publishers are willing to allow subpublishers a percentage of foreign income in the subpublisher's territory in exchange for an advance and the other available amenities.

THE COUNTRY-BY-COUNTRY APPROACH

If a U.S. publisher decides to take the country-by-country approach to subpublishing, he will be entering into a series of agreements with various subpublishers. For each agreement there will be several points of negotiation to consider.

If a song is released in the United Kingdom, the U.S. publisher will probably be contacted by several British publishers wishing to represent the song in the territory they usually cover (United Kingdom, Republic of Eire, etc.). Determining which one of these companies will act as subpublisher for the song is a process that is usually based on which company has the best reputation or which one offers the best deal. Ideally, both qualities will belong to the same company.

Some issues that should be considered by the U.S. publisher are: the amount of the advance; the term (or duration) of the subpublishing agreement; and the percentage of royalties to be retained by the subpublisher in exchange for services rendered.

Regarding the advance, the amount offered will depend on the country in question. Obviously the U.K. subpublisher will offer more than another, much less active country's subpublisher. It will be up to the U.S. publisher to determine if any of the U.K. firms are offering a reasonable advance based on recent offers to other American publishers in similar circumstances. If the U.S. publisher doesn't

Some issues that should be considered by the U.S. publisher are: the amount of the advance; the term (or duration) of the subpublishing agreement; and the percentage of royalties to be retained by the subpublisher in exchange for services rendered.

have knowledge of other recent deals, he will either have to assume that the highest offer is a reasonable advance or rely on the expertise of an entertainment lawyer who is familiar with the current advances being negotiated in the United Kingdom.

However, the highest advance doesn't necessarily dictate the best deal. The U.S. publisher must also negotiate the type of royalties the subpublisher will be able to claim and the percentages of those royalties the subpublisher will be able to retain.

According to Gary Ford, associate director of International Services for ASCAP, and former manager of foreign administration for Warner/Chappell Music, "In an ideal situation, a publisher should actually visit the office of the intended subpublisher, meet the administrative and creative staff, and get an overall feeling for how they communicate and transact business. He should check their computer systems, royalty statement formats, etc.

"Also, if the publisher wants his catalog exploited in the local market, it is often best to go with independent subpublishers as they focus primarily on exploitation of their clients' catalogs and have excellent track records for obtaining local 'covers.' [In music publishing lingo, exploitation is synonymous with plugging or promoting a song in an attempt to get it recorded and/or performed.]

"However, the independents also have a reputation for not being the best administrators; hence the reasoning for either visiting the particular office *or* relying on an attorney you can trust to choose the best independent to suit your needs."

Gary feels that these points "are equally as important as an advance when deciding to do deals on a country-by-country basis. Each publisher has different needs and an advance or rate split should not be the sole determining factor in choosing a subpublisher."

Subpublishers generally issue licenses for and collect on mechanical reproductions, synch uses, printed editions, and—sometimes—the publisher's share of performance royalties. The amount of royalties the subpublisher retains can usually be anywhere from 10 to 25 percent. If the subpublisher causes a recording to be made in his territory (this is generally referred to as a "local cover" version), he frequently is allowed to keep anywhere from 25 to 40 percent of the royalties earned on that particular release.

THE SUBPUBLISHING SCENARIO

S. Mackenzie Music Publishing Company owns the song "I Love My Dog." Mr. Mackenzie makes a subpublishing deal for his catalog with a French company in which the French subpublisher will retain 10 percent of the royalties it collects on the original American recording of "I Love My Dog" in France. The French publisher is also given the right to adapt or translate the song into French so that he can have a better opportunity to exploit the song in his country. Although the foreign language version will still be copyrighted in the name of the U.S. publisher, the French publisher will be able to retain 25 percent of the royalties on *either* the English or French version of the song if he causes a recording of it to be made in his territory.

Let's say "I Love My Dog," as recorded by the American band Herman's Mutts, is an international hit (originating in the United States). If the Mutts' recording is

PERFORMANCE ROYALTY INCOME FROM FOREIGN SOURCES

The U.S. publisher's share of foreign performance royalties is usually a point of discussion in subpublishing deals because there are two possible ways for the publisher to receive foreign performance income.

One way that payment is handled is for the subpublisher to collect the U.S. publisher's foreign performance royalties directly from the foreign performing rights society with which the subpublisher is affiliated. The subpublisher then pays the publishing company its share of foreign performance income when he accounts to the publisher for all types of royalties due.

The other possible method of payment is for the foreign performing rights society to pay the publisher's (and songwriter's) share of foreign performance royalties directly to the proper performing rights society in America. That society then pays the publisher and songwriter.

Which of these two methods is best for the publisher is open to debate. In the first case mentioned above, the subpublisher is going to get to keep a portion of the U.S. publisher's performance royalty income, which—on the surface—would appear to be a disadvantage to the publisher.

On the other hand, the publisher is more likely to receive his foreign performance royalties sooner with this method, since the foreign performing rights society is paying the publisher's performance royalties directly to the subpublisher, which in turn pays the publisher the next time royalty accountings are due.

In the second scenario, the American publisher doesn't have to lose the percentage of performance royalty income that would have been taken out by the subpublisher. The disadvantage, though, is that foreign performing rights societies generally take a long time to pay U.S. performing rights societies. It also takes time for the U.S. societies to enter all of the foreign information into their computer systems. By the time the publisher finally receives the foreign performance royalties from his affiliated U.S. performing rights society, those royalties can be monies owed from the previous year or even earlier.

In the end, if this is a negotiable deal point in the U.S. publisher's agreement with his subpublisher, the publisher will have to determine which method he prefers. Of course, the subpublisher is going to want to collect the foreign performance royalties himself, since this means more money will go into his pocket.

Meanwhile, notwithstanding the manner in which the publisher is paid performance royalties, the U.S. songwriter receives his foreign performance royalties direct from his domestic performing rights society.

released in France, that wouldn't qualify the French publisher to retain 25 percent of the royalties earned in France.

However, if the French publisher gets another act to record "I Love My Dog" (the English language version) in France, he would retain 25 percent of the mechanicals received on that local cover. The same holds true if the French publisher gets Jacques Beagle to record "J'aime mon Bow Wow"—the French version of the song.

Assuming S. Mackenzie Music Publishing Company has a contract with the writer of "I Love My Dog" that calls for the songwriter to receive 50 percent of the mechanical income received by the publisher from foreign sources, the royalty payments would go like this:

Let's say the subpublisher in France receives the equivalent of $1,000 in mechanical royalties for Herman's Mutts' recording of "I Love My Dog." According to the subpublishing agreement, he retains $100 and pays the remaining $900 to S. Mackenzie's company. S. Mackenzie then pays $450 (50 percent of the mechanical income from the foreign sources) to the writer of "I Love My Dog."

When Jacques Beagle's recording of "J'aime mon Bow Wow" becomes a hit in France, the French publisher receives another $1,000 in mechanical royalties—this time for Jacques's local cover recording of the song. The subpublisher now retains $250 (25 percent of the local cover version income) and pays $750 to S. Mackenzie. S. Mackenzie then pays $375 to the composer of "I Love My Dog" (once again, 50 percent of income from a foreign source received by the American publisher).

What about the French writer who turned "I Love My Dog" into "J'aime mon Bow Wow"? He receives mechanical royalties out of the 25 percent retained by the French publisher according to whatever deal the two of them have negotiated. He will also receive a portion of the song's performance royalty income reported in France, but only on the French language version of the song.

THE SUBPUBLISHING AGREEMENT TERM

Another area of consideration is the term of the agreement. In earlier days, subpublishers often acquired a song for the life of copyright (which, in many countries, was already "life-plus-fifty"). In some cases, subpublishers would retain the rights to a song for the first term of U.S. copyright. As you can see, if a U.S. publisher became unhappy with a particular subpublisher, the results could be pretty devastating, since the publisher would already have given the song away for either "life-plus-fifty" or for a period of at least twenty-eight years. Since the life of a copyright is now "life-plus-seventy" in many foreign countries, the U.S. publisher who entered into a "life of copyright" deal a few decades ago has lost the song outside the U.S. for twenty more years than he originally thought he would.

In more recent times, subpublishing deals have taken on more reasonable durations. Today the common subpublishing term is usually around three years. The philosophy behind the three-year term is that the subpublisher will have plenty of time to show that he can exploit the song in his market but not so much time that the remaining points of the deal have a chance to become antiquated.

There was a time when the subpublisher retained 50 percent of all income collected as opposed to the 10 to 20 percent usually retained today. Many American publishers now find themselves locked into those old 50/50 deals for the life of their copyrights because those types of deals were very common not too many years ago. Luckily for U.S. publishers and songwriters, such deals don't happen anymore when dealing with legitimate subpublishers.

Another major point of negotiation is the rights being granted to the subpublisher. We already know that the subpublisher has the right to collect mechanical, synch and print royalties (and sometimes performance royalties). However, in a normal, pro-U.S. publisher deal, the subpublisher does not acquire the copyright itself in the subpublisher's territory. The publisher is merely allowing the subpublisher to act on the publisher's behalf.

In non-English-speaking countries, as pointed out in "The Subpublishing Scenario," the American publisher will usually allow the subpublisher to have translations or adaptations of the lyrics created (to be approved by the publisher and, sometimes, the songwriter) so that the subpublisher will be in a better position to promote the song. The publisher should own the copyright to these new versions of the works; otherwise, if he decides to change subpublishers, the original subpublisher may claim to own rights to the adapted versions of the songs in the catalog. Two versions of the same song in the same country would not only be difficult to exploit, but payment of royalties would be confusing at best.

The number of songs the subpublisher acquires depends on the individual deal. A subpublisher may be granted the rights to a single song, to all of the songs the U.S. publisher acquires during the term of the subpublishing agreement, or to any or all of the songs in the publisher's catalog that haven't already been assigned to another subpublisher in a particular territory.

If a subpublisher is acquiring the rights to an American publisher's catalog that contains several hits, that publisher should be able to strike a much better deal than another American publisher who is offering only one song for subpublication.

Of course, a U.S. publisher with several hits could make deals with various subpublishers in the same territory on a song-by-song basis, acquiring advances from each subpublisher that might total more than the single advance offered by one subpublisher for all of the songs. But, once again, the U.S. publisher might find himself buried under tons of paperwork while trying to keep track of who subpublishes what song in which territory—which leads us to the other main subpublishing option available to the U.S. publisher.

In a normal deal, the subpublisher does not acquire the copyright itself. The publisher is merely allowing the subpublisher to act on the publisher's behalf.

THE SINGLE WORLDWIDE SUBPUBLISHING APPROACH

This type of agreement is usually made with a multinational subpublisher—a major publishing company that either already has subpublishing deals in place throughout the world or owns its own subpublishing companies around the globe.

Although the publisher would receive only one overall advance—as opposed to advances from each country—a major benefit of the single worldwide subpublishing agreement is that it is much simpler and easier to maintain. Also, by going with this approach, the publisher has only one deal to negotiate. And he will usually receive one foreign royalty statement twice a year that covers the entire world, rather than receiving many different statements from various territories at different times during a twelve-month period.

As Gary Ford explains, "There are many other advantages of going with a multinational subpublisher: They usually have a better working relationship with their local performing rights societies due to their size; their computer systems are normally more up to date; and their professional staff is better equipped to deal with areas not usually addressed by the independent subpublisher."

The various negotiating points of the worldwide subpublishing agreement are very similar to a single subpublishing agreement. However, the U.S. publisher has to protect himself from allowing the worldwide subpublisher to pay less than the U.S. publisher is expecting by avoiding accounting for royalties "at the source."

Sound confusing? It is. Many U.S. publishers have been duped by subpublishers with whom they have entered into worldwide agreements. Although this is not a practice among the well-known and well-respected multinational subpublishers, it does still take place among a few companies. Here's how it works:

U.S. publisher "A" enters into a worldwide subpublishing agreement with publisher "B," who owns publishing companies around the world. "B" agrees to pay "A" 80 percent of the royalties "B" receives from its subpublishers. (Remember, these are companies that "B" owns.) Meanwhile, "B" has agreements with all of its subpublishers (essentially, agreements with itself) stating that the subpublishers will retain 50 percent of all sums received in their territories. So, if English subpublisher "C" receives $200 in royalties for a song in "A"'s catalog, "C" retains $100 and sends $100 (50 percent) to "B" in the United States. "B" then pays $80 to "A". Meanwhile, "A" was expecting to receive $160 (80 percent of $200).

There are several variations on this theme, the end result of which is that publisher "A" receives substantially less subpublishing royalties than his agreement would seem to indicate. To avoid this problem—known in the industry as "double dipping"—a good entertainment lawyer makes certain that the worldwide subpublishing agreement calls for royalties to be computed "at the source." In other words, each subpublisher must report the amount earned in his territory, of which 80 percent is to be received by publisher "A" when royalties are paid.

A FINAL WORD ON SUBPUBLISHING

The amount of royalties earned abroad on an international hit originating in the United States can sometimes be as much as or more than the amount earned in this country.

Subpublishing is more important today than it has ever been before. The amount of royalties earned abroad on an international hit originating in the United States can sometimes be as much as or more than the amount earned in this country.

In the past, American publishers put the most emphasis on the amount of the advance they could get from a subpublisher without worrying about how much that song might eventually earn in a foreign territory. In fact, after the initial large advance, the publishers often left the subpublisher to his own devices.

Today subpublishers have become very competitive. Due to the shortened term of most subpublishing agreements, subpublishers work harder to exploit U.S. publishers' songs so their agreements will be renewed on a continuing basis.

Finally, it is interesting to note that the Internet might prove to be an extremely important factor in the future of subpublishing. By virtue of the fact that the World Wide Web is, indeed, worldwide, U.S. publishers are now capable of promoting their catalogs over the Internet. With that in mind, it's conceivable that the day will come when U.S. publishers will also be able to administer and collect royalties from foreign sources without the help of today's conventional subpublisher. What will happen to the entire concept of subpublishing in the years ahead depends almost entirely upon where expanding technology will lead us.

Six

THE SONGWRITER'S OPTIONS

*E*very published songwriter I have ever known has regretted at least one publishing agreement he or she has signed. In a lot of cases that regret is justified. In others, if the writer hadn't signed the contract as written (or with a minimum of changes), the song probably wouldn't have been recorded at all, and the songwriter's career might not have gotten off the ground.

The fact is, if you are an unknown, never-had-a-song-recorded songwriter, it is highly unlikely that the very first agreement you sign is going to be as favorable as the agreement a songwriter with several hits to his credit is going to sign. Keep in mind that you shouldn't necessarily expect to start your career at the top. A young college graduate seeking employment is not going to walk into the personnel office at Microsoft and apply for the president's job. It's much more likely that he's going to take the lowest position available and slowly work his way up.

Luckily, in the music business, rising to the top might not take nearly as long. But getting there is still probably going to require some compromises on your part. Your advantage will be that you will know what compromises you are making because you are about to learn what your options are. And even the subtlest difference in the type of agreement you sign can mean a significant difference in royalties earned on a hit song.

Throughout this chapter we'll discuss the various types of publishing agreements generally available to a songwriter. Let's start with the most common type of agreement between a songwriter and a publisher that exists today.

"If I had only known then what I know now, I wouldn't have signed that first contract without considering all of my options."
—Every Songwriter That Ever Lived

THE SINGLE SONG CONTRACT

The single song contract is an agreement between a music publisher and a songwriter in which the songwriter grants certain rights to a publisher for one or more songs. In acquiring these rights the music publisher usually provides an advance against future royalties and agrees to attempt to cause the song to be used in one or more ways that will cause both parties to receive income from such uses. (The phrase "single song contract" is another music publishing misnomer. One single song

Even the subtlest difference in the type of agreement you sign can mean a significant difference in royalties earned on a hit song.

contract can include several songs, all of which are individually subject to the clauses in the agreement.)

This type of agreement goes all the way back to the beginning of music publishing. In the days before radio, records, movies with sound, and television, the single song contract between writer and publisher only pertained to sheet music and the amount of money the publisher would pay the songwriter for each copy of sheet music sold.

A few years ago I was given a copy of a single song contract from the late nineteenth century. The entire contract looked something like this:

ROYALTY CONTRACT

New York, _____ 18 ____

We hereby agree to pay

_____ [author of song] _____

the sum of _____ cents (_____ per cent)

on each copy sold of a _____ [vocal or instrumental] _____

composition entitled:

_____

Settlements to be made the first day of every

_____

Signed,

_____
Publisher

Even in the late 1800s, single song contracts could be a little confusing. The particular contract I have is for four cents on each copy sold. In parentheses it says

"(10 percent)." Apparently this meant that the retail price of the sheet music was forty cents. The agreement goes on to say "settlements" will be made on January 1st and July 1st.

Ironically, there are single song contracts being written today that still call for the writer to receive as little as eight cents per copy on sheet music sales even though the retail price on sheet music is now around four dollars.

Single song contracts have undergone a lot of changes in the past century. Many single song contracts today consist of over twenty paragraphs that attempt to cover all possible types of royalties from all kinds of sources "now known or later developed."

Many songwriters complain about the length and complexities of today's single song contract. However, all of the provisions that now exist in these contracts evolved out of technological advances and precedent-setting situations that transpired over the decades.

For example, today smart songwriters insist that an audit clause be included in the single song contract. In the 1800s a publisher could tell a songwriter that one thousand pieces of sheet music were sold when the true amount was actually ten thousand. If the songwriter's contract didn't call for the right to audit the publisher's books, the songwriter would lose out on a lot of money.

So, rather than complain about the length and technical wording of a contract, the songwriter is better off learning what the single song contract is all about. A properly constructed agreement can protect both the writer and the publisher in any given situation.

A properly constructed agreement can protect both the writer and the publisher in any given situation.

Although the wording differs from one single song contract to another, most of the contracts have basic paragraphs in common regarding the advance, royalty payments, copyright ownership, writer's warrant that the song is an original work, and so on.

There is no such thing as a "Standard Song Contract," despite the fact that many publishers have contracts with the word "standard" in the heading. Any time a publisher offers a "standard contract" without allowing the songwriter the right to negotiate certain points of the agreement, it's time for the songwriter to seriously question the intentions of the publisher. (See the Appendix for a copy of The Songwriters Guild's Popular Songwriters Contract. While it's not a "standard" contract, it is very fair to writers.)

When I use the phrase "standard contract," I am merely referring to a contract that has elements in common with other contracts of that type. Here are some characteristics common to all legitimate single song contracts.

Advances

The reason a publisher wants a songwriter to sign a single song contract is because the publisher believes that he can earn income on the song through successful exploitation. In exchange for attaining certain rights to that song, the publisher should be willing to offer an advance.

If, on the other hand, the publisher asks that the songwriter pay *him*, then the songwriter isn't dealing with a true publisher. As you learned in chapter two, anyone who demands money from a songwriter to acquire publishing rights to a song is known in the industry as a "song shark." Therefore, any agreement that demands payment rather than offering an advance is not a legitimate single song contract.

This is not to say that every single song contract offers an advance to the

Anyone who demands money from a songwriter to acquire publishing rights to a song is known in the industry as a "song shark."

THE SONGWRITERS GUILD OF AMERICA

The Songwriters Protective Association (SPA) was formed in 1931 by three respected songwriters: Billy Rose ("It's Only a Paper Moon," "Me and My Shadow"); George W. Meyer ("For Me and My Gal"); and Edgar Leslie ("Moon Over Miami"). These men created SPA for the purpose of taking actions that would "advance, promote and benefit" the songwriting profession.

The following year a Standard Uniform Popular Songwriters Contract was developed by SPA for members of the organization. This contract was intended to be used by songwriters as a fairer document than the types of contracts publishers were offering to most writers at that time.

Now known as The Songwriters Guild of America (SGA), it is the largest and oldest songwriters' association in the country. SGA provides a variety of services to its members, including contract reviews, royalty collections (excluding performance royalties), audits of publishers and catalog administration. The Guild also continues to issue its own songwriter's contract, which was most recently updated in 1978 to take full advantage of the 1976 Copyright Act.

Although the word "protective" is no longer a part of the Guild's name, protection is still an important function of the association, according to its current president, songwriter George David Weiss ("Can't Help Falling in Love," "The Lion Sleeps Tonight," "What a Wonderful World"). "It is unfortunately true that we live in a far from perfect world," says Weiss. "There are people out there who are constantly seeking ways to take advantage of songwriters, to tap into the creator's almost desperate need to have his material presented to the world. This desperation makes a writer fair game for the 'song shark,' for the unscrupulous.

"The Songwriters Guild of America offers the songwriter a haven: protection against those who would victimize and cheat him or her; assurance that royalties are accurate and paid in a timely fashion; a vigorous voice in Washington, acting as our watchdog to block legislation that would harm us, and seeking passage of bills to help us."

SGA is governed by a council made up of professional songwriters. Although there are many expenses involved in the operation of the organization, the president and Guild council members are all volunteers. The expenses incurred are covered by annual membership dues and a commission charged on royalties collected from publishers on behalf of SGA members.

The Guild offers three types of membership: Associate Membership (for unpublished writers); Regular Membership (for published writers); and Special Associate Membership (for heirs of published songwriters).

More information on The Songwriters Guild of America is available by writing the association at 1500 Harbor Blvd., Weehawken, NJ 07087. The phone number is (201) 867-7603; fax number is (201) 867-7535. A copy of the Guild contract appears in the Appendix, along with an overview of the agreement's major clauses.

songwriter. A new publishing company may be too small to offer an advance. The publisher's argument might be that, since the company is small and "hungry," the publisher is going to work much harder to try to get the song cut than would a giant company that has to deal with thousands of songs and songwriters. Such an argument might be viable. Under such circumstances, though, the new publisher should be willing to offer a better overall deal than the more established publisher who is willing to write an advance check.

So what is this advance and why does the songwriter receive it? An advance is an amount of money paid to the songwriter by the publisher for allowing the publisher to own rights to a song and to share in the future royalties the song might be due.

The actual amount of the advance varies widely among publishers, so it's impossible for me to tell you a specific dollar figure. Sometimes it's $1,000; other times it's less; other times it's more. It all depends on the publisher in question and the publisher's belief in the song's hit potential. By offering an advance, the publisher is showing that he is willing to gamble real money on his ability to get your song recorded.

Whatever the amount of the advance, the total sum is recoupable according to most single song contracts. In fact, the actual phrase is usually along the lines of "a nonreturnable, recoupable advance in the amount of $ _____ ." Although that phrase seems contradictory, what it actually means is that the songwriter will receive an advance of x dollars. If the song doesn't earn any royalties for the duration of the agreement, the songwriter doesn't pay the amount of the advance back to the publisher when the agreement expires. If, on the other hand, the song gets recorded and earns back the amount of the advance or more, the publisher gets to recoup the advance, after which all other monies earned on the song are split between the publisher and the songwriter according to their agreement.

The only songwriter's royalty that the publisher can't recoup is performance royalty income, which is paid directly to the songwriter by his performing rights society. Of course, the publishing company is receiving its share of performance royalties directly as well. However, the single song contract usually states that the advance is to be recouped from the songwriter's share of income. Therefore, the publisher doesn't usually count his own performance royalty income as money earned back by the songwriter against the songwriter's advance.

Transfer of Rights

In chapter two we covered at length the five exclusive rights of the copyright owner. Generally, in a single song contract these are the rights the songwriter transfers to the music publisher in exchange for an advance, a guarantee that the publisher will make a best effort to exploit the song, and a share of approximately 50 percent of all royalties actually earned by the song.

One of the phrases commonly used in a single song contract that refers to this trade-off is "The writer hereby sells, assigns, transfers, and delivers" the copyright to the publisher. Theoretically, the writer could sell, assign and transfer each of his five exclusive rights to five separate parties. However, since massive confusion would reign in such a situation, a writer usually transfers all of his rights in a song to one particular publisher.

The exception to this rule would arise in the case of a songwriter who co-publishes a song with another co-publisher or assigns administration rights to an administrator. We will discuss these alternatives later in this chapter.

The Songwriter's Royalties

It has generally been common practice among music publishers to offer single song contracts to songwriters without a track record. Songwriters who are already successful to some degree are usually offered other types of agreements, such as those we will cover later in this chapter, and at higher royalty rates.

The royalties that are shared between the publisher and the songwriter signing the single song contract are usually split approximately 50/50. In chapter four we discussed the various types of royalties received by publishers, all of which are covered in the single song contract.

In the case of mechanical royalties, synchronization royalties, "new media" royalties and royalties received by the publisher from foreign sources, the single song contract generally calls for the songwriter to receive 50 percent of all such income. (As you learned in chapter five, the songwriter's share of foreign performance royalties are paid to the songwriter's U.S. performing rights society by the foreign society. The American society then pays the writer. In other words, the royalties received by the publisher from foreign sources don't include the songwriter's foreign performance income.) In no case should a songwriter agree to accept less than 50 percent of the income received by the publisher from these sources. [See "Royalty Splits" chart, p. 85.]

There is one area in which the publisher will usually end up with more than 50 percent of the income received. This royalty source is printed editions, in which case the songwriter is paid at one of a variety of rates depending on the type of edition in question and on whether or not the publisher also makes the printed editions or licenses rights to a print publisher. Sheet music royalties, for example, are usually paid in amounts of *x* cents for each copy sold. Although the percentage will vary according to the deal the music publisher has with the print publisher, if the single song contract calls for the writer to receive twenty cents per copy sold, and the publisher receives fifty cents per copy sold from the print publisher, then the songwriter is going to be paid less than 50 percent on sheet music royalties.

The same is true of other printed editions as well. The single song contract may offer the songwriter 10 percent of the wholesale selling price of other printed editions of the composition (such as band, orchestra and choral arrangements) when, in fact, the publisher may be making a profit of 25 percent or more of the wholesale price.

Royalties for folios can become even more confusing, since the amount paid to the writer will depend on several factors. If the publisher prints his own folios, the royalty due the writer will be based on a percentage (usually 10 to 12½ percent) of the wholesale selling price. If the publisher allows someone else to print a folio that includes the song referred to in the single song contract, the songwriter's royalties will be based on a percentage (usually 50 percent) of what the publisher receives. In either case, the amount paid to the writer will be on a pro rata basis (determined by the number of songs in the folio).

For example, if the publisher prints a folio that contains twenty songs, one of which belongs to a songwriter signed to a single song contract that calls for the writer to receive 12½ percent of the wholesale selling price, that songwriter will

By offering an advance, the publisher is showing that he is willing to gamble real money on his ability to get your song recorded.

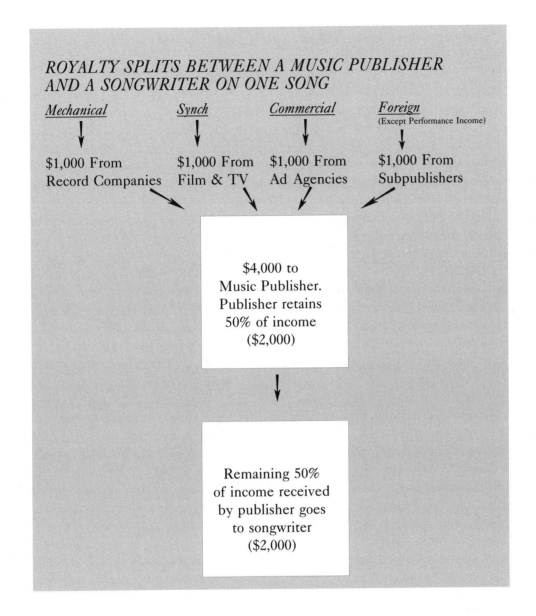

ROYALTY SPLITS BETWEEN A MUSIC PUBLISHER
AND A SONGWRITER ON ONE SONG

Mechanical → $1,000 From Record Companies

Synch → $1,000 From Film & TV

Commercial → $1,000 From Ad Agencies

Foreign (Except Performance Income) → $1,000 From Subpublishers

$4,000 to Music Publisher. Publisher retains 50% of income ($2,000)

Remaining 50% of income received by publisher goes to songwriter ($2,000)

This chart assumes that the songwriter has recouped any outstanding advances and that the publisher's single song contract calls for the writer to receive 50 percent of the royalties from the four income sources listed. Also, the foreign performance royalties (not shown) are paid to the publisher's and songwriter's U.S. performing rights society, which then pays both the writer and publisher their shares of performance royalties directly.

receive 12½ percent of one twentieth of the wholesale selling price. If the wholesale selling price is $6, the songwriter would receive 3¾ cents for each copy sold ($6 divided by 20 times 12½ percent).

On the other hand, let's say a music publisher has a print deal with a print publisher. The print publisher puts out a folio containing twelve songs, two of which belong to the music publisher. One of the two songs is written by a songwriter signed to a single song contract that calls for him to receive 50 percent of the publisher's receipts on a pro rata basis. In this case, the songwriter will receive 50 percent of half of the royalties earned by the music publisher from the folio (half of the music publisher's royalties times 50 percent).

Territory Covered

The single song contract almost always calls for the publisher to acquire worldwide rights to the song in question. This gives the publisher the greatest possible chance of earning income on the song by either adding it to the songs that are already part

The single song contract almost always calls for the publisher to acquire worldwide rights to the song in question.

of a subpublishing agreement or by assigning the song to various subpublishers throughout the world.

Term of the Contract

The "term" of the single song contract is the specific amount of time that the contract will be in effect. This length of time will be determined by several factors.

As I have said before, the act of signing a contract with a music publisher doesn't mean a song is now considered to be published. When a songwriter signs a single song contract, he is allowing one publisher to acquire the rights to one or more songs for a period of time.

Before the 1976 Copyright Act went into effect, there were generally two possible terms a songwriter could agree to: the first term of U.S. copyright (twenty-eight years) or the life of copyright including the renewal term (fifty-six years). The 1976 law changed the life of copyright to the life of the author plus fifty years, while at the same time saying that a writer can terminate an agreement with a publisher at the end of thirty-five years if the song has been published or after forty years from the date of the agreement, whichever is shorter. If the writer and/or his heirs wish, however, the song may remain with the original publisher for the rest of the copyright's life ("life-plus-fifty"). In such a case, the publisher would usually have to pay an advance or bonus (a bonus is nonrecoupable) in order to get to retain the copyright.

Of course, in a single song contract, the writer and publisher can agree to whatever amount of time they wish, up to the maximum allowed by copyright law. If Wanda the writer can convince Pete the publisher that Pete should have the song for only a decade, then the term of the single song contract would be ten years. If the contract included a "reversion clause" (see below), then the term of the contract might be even shorter.

The Reversion Clause

In the single song contract there is sometimes a specified amount of time in which the publisher is allowed to attempt to acquire a recording of the song in question. If the publisher is not successful in his efforts, all rights revert to the writer.

In the single song contract there is sometimes a specified amount of time in which the publisher is allowed to attempt to acquire a recording of the song in question. For instance, the songwriter may agree that the publisher has, say, one year to get the song cut. At the end of one year from the date of the contract, if the publisher is not successful in his efforts, all rights in the song revert to the writer. The portion of the single song contract that spells out the songwriter's right to regain the copyright is called the reversion clause. If the reversion becomes effective because the publisher hasn't caused the song to be recorded, some reversion clauses stipulate that the writer has to return the advance and/or the amount of the publisher's demo costs.

It's also important to note that the amount of the advance might depend on the length of time the publisher is allowed to try to get the song recorded. For instance, a publisher who has only six months before a reversion clause goes into effect is probably going to offer a lower advance (if any) than a publisher would who has a year or eighteen months to try to get the song used.

Another possible cause for a copyright to revert to a songwriter would be if the publisher fails to pay royalties properly or on time. Some single song contracts include this type of language as well. [See the Songwriters Guild contract in the Appendix.]

Once the song is recorded and released (and, therefore, "published" as defined by copyright law), the copyright remains with the publisher unless some action (or inaction) takes place that causes the reversion clause to go into effect.

Accounting and Audit Clauses

Earlier we covered the topic of royalties to be paid to the writer by the publisher. Elsewhere in the single song contract there is a paragraph that explains how often and at what time during the fiscal or calendar year the publisher will make these royalty payments. Generally, royalty payments will be made twice a year at six-month intervals, usually within forty-five days after the end of each six-month period. Assuming the publisher pays based on the calendar year, the writer should expect to be paid around August 14 (forty-five days after June 30) and around February 14 (forty-five days after December 31).

For the songwriter's protection there should also be an audit clause that allows the writer (or his financial representative) to examine the publisher's books once a year to make certain that royalty payments are accurate. Many publishers honestly attempt to make proper payments. Those that don't make payments on time usually develop a reputation that prevents writers from wanting to sign agreements with them in the future. Sometimes, though, publishers or their royalty departments do make mistakes, so even the most honest of publishers can, on occasion, pay a writer less than he is actually due. For this reason, a publisher should be willing to include an audit clause in the single song contract.

Warranty, Indemnity and Disputes

These three topics are all a part of the common single song contract. The "warranty" section applies to the writer, who is required to warrant (or guarantee) that he is transferring the rights in an original work of authorship to the publisher, and that he hasn't already transferred those rights to any other publisher or third party.

The indemnity clause relates directly to the warranty clause. The indemnity clause says that the writer will be held financially responsible for any lawsuits that might arise in case it turns out that, in fact, the song was actually written by someone else, or that the writer had already assigned the song to another publisher.

The "disputes" clause, on the other hand, refers to possible clashes between the writer and the publisher. Usually such disputes will transpire sometime shortly after the songwriter has had the publisher's books audited. Normally this kind of dispute will be resolved by proper payment from the publisher.

But what if the publisher refuses to pay what is obviously owed? Or what if the publisher refuses to grant an audit at all, even though the contract clearly states that he must? The disputes clause is included in the single song contract to clarify how an internal disagreement will be resolved. Usually it will state that, rather than allowing actual lawsuits to be filed, the writer and publisher will agree to a resolution of any disputes through binding arbitration. Binding arbitration is the act of settling a dispute by putting the problem before a qualified, disinterested third party who will decide how the dispute will be resolved.

THE EXCLUSIVE OR STAFF WRITER CONTRACT

The phrases "exclusive contract" or "staff writer contract" refer to an agreement in which the writer is signed exclusively to a particular publishing company.

Exclusive or staff writer contracts are two different names for the same type of agreement. In other words, if you are signed to what is referred to as an exclusive contract, you are on the writing staff of a publishing company; and if you are signed to a staff writer contract, you are working exlusively for one publisher. For the sake of brevity, let's refer to this agreement throughout this chapter as a staff writer contract.

Staff writer contracts usually come into play when a writer's past success causes a publisher to believe that the songwriter's talents warrant a deal that will allow the publisher to acquire the rights to all of the songs written by the writer during a specific period of time. Sometimes a writer's track record might consist of only one or two recorded songs.

In fact, this is usually the best time (from the publisher's point of view) to get a songwriter to sign an exclusive deal. A songwriter with no previous success and a handful of songs might be considered too much of a risk by most publishers. A writer with several hits under his belt would demand a large weekly advance and a contract heavily in his favor. However, a writer with only a cut or two to his name is the perfect type for a publisher to approach with an offer of a staff writer agreement.

A proper comparison to a staff writer contract would be that of an artist contracted to a particular record label. As long as the artist is signed to that label, he can't go out and make a record for a rival company.

A proper comparison to a staff writer contract would be that of an artist contracted to a particular record label.

Advances

One of the major differences between the single song contract and the staff writer contract is the amount of advance money involved and the manner in which the advance is paid. When a writer signs a single song contract, he is paid a one-time, recoupable advance. In the case of the staff writer, an advance is paid weekly, monthly or—in rarer instances—quarterly. A staff writer can sometimes earn a weekly draw (which is, of course, actually a recoupable advance) equal to the amount of the advance for a single song contract. The amount will usually depend on the writer's negotiating power.

For example, a nonperforming songwriter with a minimal number of recorded songs generally has very little negotiating power. He is probably looking for a publisher willing to sign him to a staff writer agreement for a few hundred dollars a week so that he can make ends meet for the duration of the agreement while he writes full time.

On the other hand, a writer who also has a recording contract will be offered a very high advance (a thousand dollars or much more per week). The publishing company knows that it has an excellent chance of recouping the advance and making a profit off of an agreement with a writer/performer, since the writer is already planning to release an album filled entirely with his own songs.

Somewhere in between these two plateaus is the writer/performer who hasn't yet acquired a recording contract. As I have emphasized before, music publishing is no longer just a matter of finding a great song and trying to get it recorded. Granted, this is still an important part of the business, especially in Nashville. However, many music publishers (including those in Nashville) are on the lookout for the songwriter/performer who can be taken into the recording studio where professional artist demos or even finished masters of the songwriter's original material can be made. The music publisher then pitches the finished product to record labels in an attempt to turn the performing songwriter into a recording star. Thus, the publisher will often sign the writer/artist to a staff writer contract and attempt to get a recording contract for him so that the publisher will, once again, be in a position to reap a profit from such a situation.

Publishers are almost always open to signing a writer who has a built-in guarantee that his songs will be recorded. This can come in the form of the possibilities mentioned above (a writer/artist signed or about to be signed to a recording contract) or of a songwriter who is also a record producer with the power to get his own songs cut.

Of course, as I said earlier, writers in these positions can demand a great deal of money and a staff writer contract with terms very favorable to the writer. As we will see, writers in such powerful positions are much more likely to sign copublishing or administration agreements than staff writer agreements, which generally grant all of the publisher's share of income to the publisher offering the staff writer deal.

Term of the Staff Writer Contract

In staff writer agreements, there are generally three types of terms involved. The first of these three is the term of the staff writer contract. This is usually a one-year term with a specific series of one-year options. For example, if a contract calls for a one-year deal with three one-year options, this means the publisher has the option to decide if he wishes to continue his relationship with the writer at the end of each year, for a total contractual term of four years (the original one-year term plus the three options).

The term of the staff writer contract is usually a one-year term with a specific series of one-year options.

The second type of term is the length of time the publisher will retain ownership of the copyrights acquired during the duration of the staff writer contract. In some cases this will be the same as in a single song contract (approximately thirty-five years). In many modern-day staff writer agreements, publishers have agreed to shorter terms of five to twenty-five years. At the end of this term, the copyright reverts to the writer, who can sign a new deal with the publisher, assign the copyright to another publisher or assign the copyright to his own publishing company.

The third term is the amount of time the publisher is allowed to try to get the songs in question recorded. Often this term will be the length of the staff writer agreement plus anywhere from one to five years. If there are songs that remain unrecorded after that time, many staff writer agreements allow the writer to "buy back" those copyrights for the amount of any unrecouped advances and the costs of the demos of the unrecorded songs.

Works Made for Hire

As I mentioned in chapter two, a "work made for hire" is "a work prepared by an employee within the scope of his or her employment. . . ." Some publishers concur that songs written by a staff writer are works made for hire, thereby claiming actual authorship of the work as the employer (the publisher) under the copyright law. In these publishers' staff writer agreements, language is usually included stating that all songs written during the term of the agreement will be considered works made for hire. Despite the fact that the copyright law says the employer will be considered the author of a work made for hire, the publisher will usually agree to

Some publishers concur that songs written by a staff writer are works made for hire, thereby claiming actual authorship of the work as the employer (the publisher) under the copyright law.

credit the writer in the appropriate instances and allow the writer to receive the usual writer's share of all types of royalties.

However, the copyright wouldn't revert to the writer at the end of thirty-five years since the copyright law clearly states that the employer is considered to be the author. A songwriter who is offered a staff writer agreement should try to have such language removed from the agreement. In fact, the writer should ask that the contract specifically state that any songs written during the term are *not* works made for hire. Of course, the publisher may insist that the work-for-hire language stays, in which case the writer will have to accept the situation if he signs the agreement.

Other Points Common to the Staff Writer Contract
Most of the other topics covered in the staff writer contract are similar in nature to those in a single song contract. A couple of other items common to the staff writer agreement are: 1) a specific number of songs required to be written and 2) inclusion of back catalog.

A staff writer deal will usually require that the writer turn over to the publisher a certain number of acceptable songs each year.

1. A staff writer deal will usually require that the writer turn over to the publisher a certain number of acceptable songs each year. The number of songs will vary depending on the writer. However, the number of songs the writer agrees to turn out may affect the amount of advance money he is offered. Also, it's important to note that the number of songs doesn't mean exactly what it might seem.

   If a writer agrees to write twenty songs a year, he is agreeing that his share of the writing will total twenty complete songs. In other words, if that writer composes the melody to twenty songs for which someone else writes the lyrics, he has only written the equivalent of ten complete songs. He will have to write either twenty more melodies or ten more songs that are written solely by him, or some variation of the two, so that the total amount of songs for the year will equal twenty complete songs.

   A couple of paragraphs back I slipped in the phrase "a certain amount of *acceptable* songs each year." What this means is that the songs presented to the publisher must be deemed acceptable material by him. If a writer submits a song the publisher considers to be too weak to try to exploit, the writer will not be able to count it against the total number of songs required in his contract. Of course, the exception would be if the writer is also a recording artist. If he records the song and it's released on an album, it will obviously count in the total number of songs, no matter how bad the publisher might think it is.

2. The other topic common to staff writer agreements involves the writer's back catalog. These are songs written prior to signing the staff writer contract. Often a writer will agree to include these titles if they are available and if they will count against the total number of songs required by the agreement. However, the writer obviously can't agree to include songs that are already signed to another publisher. Also, if the writer owns the publishing to a song that has already been successfully recorded, he is not likely to want to give up that song to another publisher.

COPUBLISHING

Copublishing means exactly what the word implies: two or more publishers co-owning the rights in a particular song or group of songs. There are several different situations that would cause a song to be copublished.

For example, a successful songwriter may be offered a staff writer contract with a large advance in exchange for splitting the publisher's share with the established publisher who is offering the deal. In other words, the established publisher will own 50 percent of the publisher's share of income (as opposed to 100 percent) and will allow the writer to own the remaining 50 percent of the publisher's share (along with 100 percent of the writer's share). This type of agreement has become very commonplace in recent years. (As I have said before, why should a writer—and especially a successful writer or a writer/performer—grant all of the publisher's share of income to an outside party?)

For his 50 percent interest in the publisher's share, the established publisher will usually handle all of the administrative and professional duties. When royalties are due, the writer/publisher will receive 75 percent of the income (all of the writer's share and half of the publisher's share), and the established publisher will retain 25 percent (his half of the publisher's share).

Another type of copublishing situation can occur when two writers each own the publishing on their share of a song they have written together. In this case the

A successful songwriter may be offered a staff writer contract with a large advance in exchange for splitting the publisher's share with the established publisher who is offering the deal.

MUSIC PUBLISHING MATH

Just as music publishing seems to have a language all its own, this profession also appears to have made up its own form of math. For the uninitiated this math can be confusing, since the total percentage of the publisher's and songwriter's shares on a particular song can be either 100 or 200 percent, depending on the type of royalty being discussed and who's discussing it.

Some forms of royalty income are referred to on a basis of 100 percent. This is because the publisher (assuming there are no copublishers) receives 100 percent of the income from a particular source (such as mechanical royalties from a record company) and then divides the income between himself and the songwriter(s). The most common percentages for a song with one publisher and two writers would be referred to as indicated on the first pie chart on the next page.

In the case of performance royalties, however, the performing rights societies pay the publisher(s) and songwriter(s) their individual shares directly. A publisher who has no copublisher(s) on a particular song receives a statement saying that he is receiving 100 percent of the publisher's share of the performance royalties for that song. The songwriter of that same song (assuming there is only one writer) receives a statement which also says 100 percent.

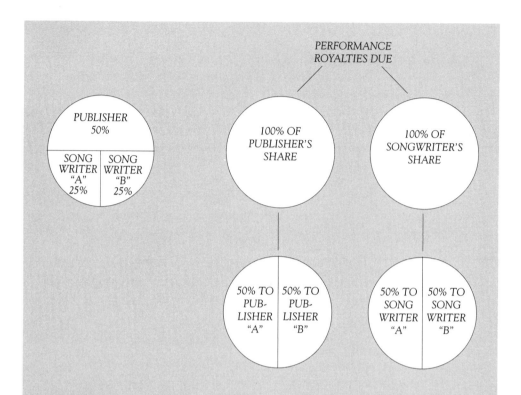

When a publisher and a songwriter of a particular song receive performance royalty statements that indicate payments of less than 100 percent for each, this means that there is more than one publisher and more than one writer of that song. The four pie charts above and on the right indicate that a performing rights society is paying royalties for a song with two co-publishers and two songwriters.

When you add up the publishers' and songwriters' shares of performance royalty income, the total comes to 200 percent. Although this is a simple concept, there is a natural tendency among those of us who believe that it's hard to have more than 100 percent of something to be confused when these strange percentages start to be discussed.

Perhaps the best way to look at this is from the songwriter's perspective. If you write half of a song and someone else writes the other half, you are going to take credit for 50 percent of the writing. If your song is published by an outside publisher, however, you're likely to receive only 25 percent of the income. So, if you add up your 50 percent, your partner's 50 percent, and your publisher's 100 percent of the publisher's share, you're back to 200 percent again. Welcome to the world of music publishing math.

two writers will: 1) each administer his own publishing company; 2) determine which of the two publishing companies will act as administrator; or 3) hire an outside administrator. [See "Administration Agreements," p. 93.]

If two writers who wrote songs together were signed to the same publisher, and one of the writers regained his share of the copyrights upon renewal (or for some contractual reason) while the other writer remained with the original publisher, there would now be two copublishers co-owning the songs written together by the two writers.

Now let's say two writers are signed to staff writer agreements with two separate publishers. If these two writers (both of whom have copublishing agreements) decide to write a song together, there would then be four copublishers of that song. Keeping track of proper payments on such a song may seem a cumbersome task, but it's not uncommon. There is one song among the catalogs I have managed that has nine copublishers. I have heard of songs that have even more.

The percentage a copublisher owns depends entirely on the situation at hand. The most common is an equal split between copublishers. The manner in which royalties are disbursed among the copublishers depends on the agreement (if any) entered into by the parties. For instance, in some cases the copublishers draw up an agreement stating that one of the two (or more) copublishers will administer the copyright(s) in question. What this usually means is that one specific copublisher will handle all of the licensing and collection of royalties and will then pay the amount due to the other copublisher(s) on a quarterly or semiannual basis. The copyright law says that if there is no written agreement between the copublishers, either or any of them can enter into a nonexclusive license as long as the other copublishers are properly accounted to.

In other words, if a copyright is owned by copublisher "A" and copublisher "B," copublisher "A" can make a deal for the song to be used in a movie for $100,000 as long as copublisher "A" then pays copublisher "B" his share of the $100,000 or has the film company pay copublisher "B" his share directly.

If, on the other hand, an ad agency wants to use a song in a commercial exclusive to a particular product (e.g., dog food), should there be no written agreement between the copublishers, all of the copublishers would have to jointly agree to that exclusive use. Each copublisher would then collect his share of the synch royalties directly from the party to whom the synch license was issued.

The important thing to note is that copublishing is very much a part of the music business today. The manner in which all of the parties involved are going to be collecting their shares of royalties due must be agreed upon either via an agreement among all of the parties or by adherence to the copyright law.

ADMINISTRATION AGREEMENTS

An administration agreement is an arrangement that usually takes place between an administrator and a songwriter who owns 100 percent of the publishing on his songs. As I mentioned above, two songwriters who co-own the publishing rights to a song or songs may want to use an outside administrator as well.

Joan Schulman is a well-known music publishing executive based in Los Angeles. She is currently vice president in charge of administration and licensing for the PolyGram Music Publishing Group. In the past, she has acted as an independent administrator for various songwriter/publishers. As Joan explains, "The independent administrator does all of the paperwork just like a publisher would do: files copyright and renewal registrations; issues mechanical licenses; negotiates synch fees and issues synch licenses. The independent administrator also monitors the incoming payments. If a mechanical license is issued, for instance, the administrator makes sure that the money comes in when it's due. If it doesn't, it's the administrator's responsibility to make phone calls or send letters to follow up and make sure the money is paid.

"In fact, an independent administrator does almost everything that a publisher would do except exploitation. After all, the title is 'administrator,' so it's not usually the independent administrator's job to shop songs."

An administration deal can be made between a songwriter/publisher and an independent administrator or between a writer/publisher and another music publisher who handles the administrative duties of that writer/publisher, as well as handling the administration of the music publisher's own catalog.

The administrator usually doesn't participate in copyright ownership of the writer/publisher's songs. Instead, administrators charge either a percentage (around 10 to 15 percent of the gross on royalties received) or an hourly fee for their services.

In either case, the administrator usually doesn't participate in copyright ownership of the writer/publisher's songs. Instead, administrators charge either a percentage (around 10 to 15 percent of the gross on royalties received) or an hourly fee for their services.

THE ENTERTAINMENT LAWYER

Throughout the centuries lawyers have been dealt with rather harshly. Even the Bible has some unkind things to say about them ("Woe unto you also, ye lawyers. . . ." Luke 11:46). A common complaint in the music industry has been that lawyers have taken over the business—either by running the business from behind the scenes or by actually being the heads of major music publishing and record companies. As one well-known songwriter/publisher once editorialized, there was a time when a member of the music industry would go to an entertainment attorney to get advice on how a company should be structured; at some point along the way, the lawyers stopped giving advice and just started running the companies themselves. Although the fact that lawyers seem to have too much control over the industry may anger some, it is certainly advantageous to the songwriter who is trying to get the best possible protection and the best possible deal for his songs to have a good entertainment lawyer on his side.

No matter what stage in his career a songwriter has reached, an entertainment lawyer is the only type to use. Real estate and divorce lawyers just won't do in the music business game (the former will probably be needed if you become successful; the latter will probably be needed if you become *too* successful.) An experienced entertainment lawyer knows what standard practices are in the music industry and is able to help his songwriter clients through every legal aspect of a music publishing deal.

In an ideal world (to use a common lawyer's phrase) there would be no need for lawyers. But almost everyone involved in the music business would agree that things aren't exactly ideal out there. I cannot overemphasize the lawyer's importance.

The best advice I can give on how to choose the right entertainment lawyer is to get recommendations from songwriters who are happy with their legal representation. If you don't know any successful songwriters, you should attend music industry workshops and seminars and ask the panelists for the names of respected lawyers in the business.

Rupert Holmes has strong feelings about the importance of entertainment lawyers: "I had a tendency in my first few years in the business to literally sign anything that was put in front of me. I was so afraid that I would offend someone by asking to read the contract or by taking it to a lawyer.

"I was so terrified that publishers might forever ignore me and that I would insult them so much. And, frankly, most of the time publishers have said, 'Oh, why do you want to take it to a lawyer? Lawyers cause trouble.'

"There's usually a reason why publishers say that. If someone says, 'Ah, don't bring a lawyer into this thing because it'll just get so complicated and it'll cause problems'—it means that in some way you're getting ripped off.

"If people object to you taking a contract to a lawyer, it isn't just because lawyers might make things complicated. It's because lawyers have a tendency to ask for things that might be appropriate.

"But there's still always that pressure to sign because you're afraid that the publisher will vanish. In this day and age, though, there really is no reason to rush that signature. If someone asks my advice, I just tell them to go slow in terms of signing because when you sign contracts, those signatures don't go away—and they can loom large later on."

No matter what stage in his career a songwriter has reached, an entertainment lawyer is the only type to use.

Rupert says there is another important reason to have a good entertainment lawyer: "Most of my best breaks in the business have come from attorneys and recording engineers. Choose your attorney very carefully. If you choose an attorney who's already negotiating with a major record label or publisher for five other artists that they want, and he says, 'By the way, while I'm here, would you listen to this cassette?', it can be a real good 'in' for you."

Lawyers aren't cheap. Perhaps that's one of the reasons they have to endure so much criticism. However, the amount of money they can keep you from losing will usually justify the expense of their fees.

Call them a necessary evil or a godsend, one of the most important lessons you can learn from these pages is to get the best entertainment lawyer you can afford. In fact, if you learn nothing else from this book than to hire a good entertainment lawyer before you sign that first contract (or that next contract), then I believe the cost of this book will have been worth it to you.

Seven

INSIDE THE MUSIC PUBLISHING COMPANY

$\mathcal{P}$ublishing companies come in all sizes. As you will see in the next chapter, it is possible to run a small publishing operation all by yourself. Slightly larger companies may need anywhere from three to twelve people, while a major publishing enterprise may have scores of employees located around the world.

In recent years, as large companies have become larger and larger through acquisitions and mergers, there are fewer and fewer companies that fall into the category of the "major music publisher." Most publishing companies today are of the smaller variety, consisting of a handful of employees.

No matter what size the company is, there are certain functions that a publishing enterprise must undertake to be fully operational. These functions are divided up into several departments:

1. Creative
2. Licensing
3. Copyright
4. Legal and Business Affairs
5. Print
6. Foreign
7. Royalty
8. Accounting

Each song in the publishing company has a life of its own, and must receive proper attention if it is to reach its full potential.

Overseeing this group of departments is the director of operations. In extremely large publishing companies, there may even be more than one director of operations. In fact, each department may have a director who reports to the general manager who reports to the president or chief executive officer. Sometimes there are two or three top executives in the company who are on equal ground, making group decisions rather than having one person who dictates all of the major decisions to his or her subordinates. How a publishing company is managed depends on the overall structure of the organization. Simply put, most publishing companies have one or more persons who oversee the operations and who make policy decisions.

If this all seems a bit unwieldy, it is. However, each song in the publishing company has a life of its own, and each of those songs must receive proper attention if it is to reach its full potential. Therefore, it can take many people to run a company that owns thousands of copyrights.

THE CREATIVE DEPARTMENT

The department primarily responsible for seeing that each song gets a fair chance of reaching that full potential is the creative department. (In some companies this department is known as the professional or A&R* department.) Depending on the size of the company, the creative department can be one person handling all of the creative duties or several people with their own areas of specialization or group of staff songwriters they are responsible for.

The head of the department is usually called the "creative manager." The creative manager and his staff have several specific responsibilities. Among the most important are signing songs and/or staff writers and getting songs recorded.

The creative manager is responsible for being able to "hear" a songwriter's talent or a song's hit potential. Most creative managers want to find writers they can work with over a long period of time. A dependable songwriter who continually creates commercial songs is an extremely important asset capable of helping to create a very valuable catalog for a company.

Aside from finding talented writers, it is often the creative manager's job to negotiate exclusive staff writer deals on behalf of the publishing company. Like a hip used car salesman, the creative manager has to play both ends of the deal—fighting for the writer to get the most advance money he can, yet remaining a company man and letting the writer know when he's gotten the best deal he's going to get. After these preliminary discussions, the attorneys for the publishing company and the songwriter work out the details of the staff writer contract.

Once a staff writer is on board, it's the job of the creative manager (or a member of the creative staff) to nurture the songwriter's talent through encouragement, praise, enthusiasm and anything else it takes to get the writer to create the kind of material the creative department is looking for. Frequently the writer will be teamed up with a partner or various partners (sometimes other staff writers) in an attempt to find the formula that results in the best songs.

The song plugger has an extremely important role in the creative department. As you may recall from chapter one, song plugging goes all the way back to the days before Tin Pan Alley. The song plugger is obligated to know everybody in the entertainment business who might possibly be the link to getting a song used or recorded. It is the plugger's job to see that songs belonging to the publishing company are brought to the attention of record company A&R persons, artists' lawyers, managers, record producers or the artists themselves.

Due to the enormous success of movie soundtracks such as "The Bodyguard," "Forrest Gump" and earlier films like "Purple Rain," "Dirty Dancing" and "Saturday Night Fever," many creative departments have staff members who specialize in developing contacts within the film industry, making every effort to see to it

The creative manager and his staff have the responsibilities of signing songs and/or staff writers and getting songs recorded.

It is the plugger's job to see that songs belonging to the publishing company are brought to the attention of record company A&R persons, artists' lawyers, managers, record producers or the artists themselves.

---

*"A&R" stands for "artists and repertoire." The A&R person at a record company is responsible for finding and signing artists to the record label. Similarly, the A&R person at a publishing company is responsible for finding and signing songwriter/artists to the publishing company, and then trying to get an A&R person at a record company to sign that songwriter/artist to that A&R person's label.

that songs from their catalog get included in movies that use a lot of pop, rock or country songs in their soundtracks or in television shows that feature popular music.

Another function of the creative department is to find songwriter/performers with whom development deals can be made. Although some publishing companies refer to their entire creative staff as the A&R department, other companies have specific members of the creative staff who are assigned the "A&R" title. It is the A&R men and women's job to frequent nightclubs in search of acts with original material who can be signed to the publishing company. Once the act is signed, artist demos are made and shopped to record companies in an effort to acquire recording contracts for the songwriter/performers.

THE LICENSING DEPARTMENT

The licensing department is responsible for negotiating and issuing licenses.

The licensing department is responsible for negotiating and issuing licenses. In chapter four we covered mechanical, synchronization and "new media" licenses. Depending on how any particular publishing company is set up, issuing mechanical licenses can be the domain of either the licensing department or the copyright department. However, synchronization and "new media" licenses are definitely the domain of the licensing department. In a really large publishing company, there might be one person in charge of movie licensing, another responsible for commercial licensing, another who handles TV licenses and a fourth person who just does "new media" licensing.

If the publishing company is aggressive about licensing, there may even be people on staff who are responsible for going out and drumming up business by approaching advertising agencies. For instance, the publisher of "I Love My Dog" might send out a member of the licensing department to all of the advertising agencies who have dog food manufacturers as clients. It is that person's job to try to convince the ad agencies to sell their clients on the idea of using "I Love My Dog" as the perfect song for their next commercial.

As you can see, despite the different names of the publishing company's departments, the job of the creative department and the licensing department can sometimes overlap, since the goal of every publisher is to exploit the songs in his catalog.

In the case of television shows, commercials and films, much of the time the producers decide what songs they want to use without any outside help from the publisher. As I demonstrated in the scenarios in chapter four, if the publishing company is large enough, usually all the licensing department has to do is sit back and wait for the phone to ring. When a call comes in from an ad agency, a music clearance organization, the Harry Fox Agency, a film company or the production company of a television show, it is the job of the licensing department to negotiate a fee for the use of the song. Once the fee has been negotiated, a license is sent out by the licensing department stipulating the points that have been agreed upon.

The licensing department also handles grand rights usages. If a song in the catalog is going to be included in a live theatrical presentation, the licensing department will negotiate a nightly or weekly fee to be paid, often based on a percentage of the gross box office receipts.

THE MUSIC PUBLISHING CAPITALS:
LOS ANGELES, NEW YORK AND NASHVILLE

Although there are music publishing companies throughout the United States, the three undisputed music capitals in this country are Los Angeles, New York City and Nashville. Every publishing company in these three cities has its own way of conducting business, but each of the music capitals' publishers seem to have traits indigenous to that city.

According to Steve Day, vice president of business affairs and administration for MCA Music in Nashville, "There have been many people who have made the observation that Nashville is now the Tin Pan Alley that New York once was. Nashville is now the 'Brill Building' if you will. It's become a mecca for songwriters."

New York and Los Angeles, in general, seem to have a different approach to the publishing business than Nashville has. Greg Sowders, Director, Creative for Warner/Chappell Music in Los Angeles, says the tendency in New York and L.A. is to sign writer/performers. "L.A. and New York are mostly about signing artist/writers and producer/writers, as opposed to regular, old-fashioned songwriters. This is especially true with the R & B scene on both coasts, where it seems like artists and publishers alike get their songs from producer/writers.

"I don't really find wild differences between L.A. and New York, except that the film and TV scene is more favorable to L.A., whereas New York seems to be more fertile in the area of commercials because of the ad agencies there and in Chicago.

"I'm based in L.A., but I work in New York a couple of weeks a year. When I go there, I see different faces, but I still do the same things I do in L.A. It's when I go to Nashville that I know I'm in another world.

"The art of song plugging is probably a lot healthier in Nashville than it is in L.A. or New York. It's a place where a lot of artists are still looking for material. And, it's a place where smaller publishers can exist more easily. It's not just the megacorporations running the show there. You can be a guy who runs a catalog of twenty-five songs. If one hits, it makes the same kind of money that one of those songs signed to a major publisher makes."

As far as a new writer is concerned, Steve reports that a songwriter who is signing his first deal in Nashville is likely to have to grant 100 percent of the publisher's share to establish music publisher. Greg says that most young songwriters in New York and L.A. are usually offered copublishing deals, even if they've never had a song recorded before.

However, they both agree that once a writer is so well established that he or she doesn't need an outside publisher at all, publishers in all three music capitals will jump at the chance to enter into an administration deal with that writer, providing administrative services in exchange for a small percentage of the income the writer's songs are generating.

THE COPYRIGHT DEPARTMENT

Overlapping with the licensing department is the copyright department. It is sometimes the copyright department's job to negotiate and issue mechanical licenses. Some publishing companies have at least a dozen different types of synch licenses, but there are only a couple of types of mechanical licenses: the standard mechanical license, which can be adapted to the particular rate granted (statutory, three-quarters, two-thirds, etc.), and the "controlled composition" mechanical license. This latter license is used when an artist is bound by a controlled composition clause in his recording contract. [See chapter eight, p. 109.]

Some of the other responsibilities of the copyright department are: 1) filing various forms and documents with the Copyright Office; 2) keeping track of copyright transfers from one publishing company to another; 3) keeping the royalty department apprised of new songs that have become a part of the catalog or of old songs that have undergone a change in ownership; and 4) acting as liaison with the performing rights societies.

When a song is signed to a publishing company, or when a song is written by a staff writer, the copyright department must register the new work with the Copyright Office. In the case of songs written prior to 1978 (although it is no longer mandatory), the copyright department will almost always file a Form RE (renewal) during the twenty-eighth year of copyright. Also, if there is a new version of a song, another Form PA must be filed.

If a song "changes hands," the copyright department must notify the licensees and the royalty department regarding where payments should now go and must file a copyright assignment with the Copyright Office. Let's say the song "Doowop Donna" was written in 1960. In 1988 the copyright department filed Form RE with the Copyright Office in Washington, DC. On January 1, 1989, the song went into renewal. As you learned earlier, this renewal term currently is for forty-seven years. If the original song contract from 1960 didn't grant renewal rights to the original publisher, the song would not automatically belong to the original publisher as of January 1, 1989. Nor would it continue to belong to the original publisher if the songwriter died during the first twenty-eight-year term of copyright.

If the songwriter didn't survive the first term, the rights to the song would revert to the heirs of the songwriter's estate at the end of the first term of copyright. If there were two writers on a song, and one writer died during the first term, the deceased writer's share would revert to his heirs at the end of the first copyright term. If the second writer survived the first term of copyright, and the original contract had granted renewal rights to the publisher, the publisher would have the right to retain the publishing on the second writer's share.

However, let's assume that the writer of "Doowop Donna" lived, but that the original songwriter's contract didn't grant renewals to the publisher. This being the case, the original publisher met with the writer of "Doowop Donna" in 1987 and offered him a large advance if he would agree to allow the publisher to become a copublisher of the song with the writer's own publishing company upon renewal. Let's say the writer agreed to the copublishing offer but stipulated, "My publishing company must be paid directly from the licensees for my share."

It is the job of the copyright department to inform the licensees (all of the companies currently using the song "Doowop Donna") that there are now two publishers of the song, each owning 50 percent of the publisher's share. The original publisher is to be paid one-fourth of the royalties due, and the writer's publishing company is to be paid the remaining three-fourths. (In case the math is getting a little confusing, the reason the splits are not half and half is because the writer is receiving half of the publisher's share and all of the writer's share. The original publisher, now known as one of the two copublishers, receives only half of the publisher's share. Thus, 25 percent of the royalties go to the co-publisher and 75 percent of the royalties go to the copublisher/writer.)

THE LEGAL AND BUSINESS AFFAIRS DEPARTMENT

The agreement between the original publisher of "Doowop Donna," the songwriter, and the songwriter's publishing company would be drawn up by the legal and business affairs department. Once again, depending on the size of the publishing company, the legal and business affairs department would consist of one or more lawyers and the other personnel usually associated with a law office. If the company is small- to medium-sized, there might not be an in-house legal and business affairs department. All of the legal work in a smaller publishing company is usually handled by an outside law firm that consists of one or more entertainment lawyers.

All of the legal work in a smaller publishing company is usually handled by an outisde law firm that consists of one or more entertainment lawyers.

As you discovered in chapter two, music publishing is based on the Copyright Act. It is the job of the legal and business affairs department to keep the publishing company up to date on the latest changes in the copyright law, as well as any judgments handed down that might affect the way the company conducts business.

When a new publishing company is formed, the publisher wants to have single song contracts and exclusive staff writer contracts created that are in the publisher's favor. Over the years, many variations on the "standard song contract" have been created by lawyers. It is the obligation of the legal and business affairs department to be sure that each contract has the necessary clauses and legalese to protect the interests of the publishing company.

Once the contracts have been created, the legal and business affairs department must be prepared to let the publisher know how much leeway is advisable before a contract being negotiated will tilt away from favoring the publisher and lean toward favoring the songwriter.

The responsibilities of the legal and business affairs department include: 1) developing all of the types of contracts and licenses to be used by the publishing company; 2) working with the creative department in the negotiation of any particular contract; 3) defending the publishing company when lawsuits arise (or acting as liaison to other lawyers who actually handle the litigation); 4) overseeing the filing of lawsuits when there appears to be sufficient evidence that a copyright infringement has occurred; and 5) keeping the publishing company within legal boundaries in any given situation.

THE PRINT DEPARTMENT

Like the legal and business affairs department, the print department of a publishing company will be in-house only if the size of the publishing company allows for it. Very few publishers today have their own print departments. For the most part, today's copyright-owning publishing companies "farm out" their print work to

Very few publishers today have their own print departments. Most publishing companies "farm out" their print work to print publishers who specialize.

print publishers who specialize in printing sheet music, folios, band and choral arrangements and any other types of printed editions of songs.

Whether the print department is in-house or not, it is the job of the copyright-owning publishing company to authorize the printing of music and the job of the print department or print publisher to account to the royalty department regarding the amount of printed music that has been sold.

THE FOREIGN DEPARTMENT

The duties of the foreign department can vary widely. As chapter five explained, there are publishing companies that own their own publishing companies outside of the United States; there are companies that have subpublishing agreements with foreign publishers; there are U.S. companies that have subpublishing administration deals with other domestic publishers who fit into one of the two categories mentioned above; and there are publishers who fall into other categories of foreign representation. In any of these cases, the foreign department oversees the activities of the publishing catalog outside of the United States and to take whatever action is necessary to keep the foreign operation running smoothly.

And just as subpublishers represent the U.S. publisher abroad, the U.S. publisher frequently acts as subpublisher to foreign publishing companies. Although all of the publishing company's departments are responsible for representing the foreign publishers' catalogs, the foreign department usually acts as liaison between the American publisher and its foreign affiliates.

THE ROYALTY DEPARTMENT

The royalty department determines how much is owed to all of the various parties who participate in the income of each song.

The work of all of the other departments in a publishing company points toward the royalty department. The royalty department staff is responsible for keeping track of all of the money that has come in and gone out regarding each and every song owned, co-owned, administered or subpublished by the publisher. The royalty department determines how much is owed to all of the various parties who participate in the income of each song.

For example, if a song has two publishers and three writers, the royalty departments of both of those publishers have to know who is responsible for paying each of the writers. Whatever the scenario, the royalty department generates statements and checks that are sent out to all parties who are owed royalties. These statements and checks are issued semiannually, quarterly or in whatever manner has been dictated by agreements among all of the parties involved.

THE ACCOUNTING DEPARTMENT

Accountants noted for their excellent money management skills can often reach top management positions in publishing companies without knowing even one of the songs in the publishing company's catalog.

Although it is not necessarily an in-house function (once again, depending on the size of the company), one other department that is necessary to almost all businesses is the accounting department. Because of the nature of today's publishing business, it is often the accountants who—along with lawyers—rise to the top of the larger music publishing empires. This is probably prompted by the fact that these larger publishing entities are public companies owned by stockholders who expect to see higher profits posted each year. Accountants noted for their excellent money management skills can often reach top management positions in publishing companies without knowing even one of the songs in the publishing company's catalog.

THE PUBLISHING COMPANY SCENARIO

Rover Doberman has written a song called "Doghouse Blues." He takes it to S. Mackenzie Music Publishing Company because he knows how successful the company was with their last hit, "I Love My Dog."

A member of the creative department listens to the song and thinks it has potential, although a few of the lines are a little weak and the melody could use some more variation.

The creative department staff member plays "Doghouse Blues" for the creative manager. The creative manager agrees that the song is very good but needs a little work. Since Rover doesn't have any more material prepared to play for the publishing company and no previous hits, the creative manager decides to offer Rover a single song contract rather than a staff writer deal.

"I'd like to sign your song," he tells Rover, "but I think it needs some rewriting. I'd like to let one of our staff writers take a crack at polishing it up. Of course, that means you'll have to allow him to share writer credits and royalties with you."

"You mean the writers' royalties will be split 50/50?" Rover asks.

"Not necessarily. It depends on how much the song is revised. But I guarantee you'll retain at least 50 percent of the writer's share."

Rover thinks for a moment and says, "Have the contract drawn up and sent to my lawyer."

The creative manager asks the legal and business affairs department to issue the company's standard single song contract with an additional clause stating that there will be a co-writer on the song who will receive no more than 50 percent of the writers' share of royalties resulting from income earned on the composition.

Once the contract has been drawn up, it is sent to Rover's lawyer. The lawyer finds several changes he would like to see made in the agreement. Most of them are minor, but when he comes to the clause about the co-writer, he calls Rover and says, "I think it would be in your best interest to insist that the co-writer receive only 25 percent of the writers' share unless he changes half of the song, in which case 50 percent would be acceptable." Rover agrees.

The lawyer then sends the suggested contract changes back to the legal and business affairs department. After consulting with the creative manager, the legal and business affairs department contacts Rover's lawyer, agreeing to change the co-writer clause as he requested. Other minor points are worked out, including Rover's approval of the final version of the song.

Once Rover has signed the contract, the creative manager turns Rover's song over to a staff writer named Fido Dachshund. Fido makes a few changes and—with Rover's approval—the song is finished.

A member of the creative department takes Rover, Fido and a group of musicians into a recording studio where a demo of the song is made.

Cassettes and lead sheets of the demo are then given to the creative and copyright departments. The creative department staff begins discussing who might be the right act to perform the song, while a member of the copyright department fills out a Form PA and sends it to the Copyright Office for registration.

A few weeks later a member of the creative department finds out that a band called Spot and His 102 Dalmatians are in the studio and are in need of a few more songs to finish their current album. He plays "Doghouse Blues" for the group and they agree to record it.

A short while later, Spot and His 102 Dalmatians' record company requests a mechanical license for "Doghouse Blues." The licensing department (or copyright department, depending on the company's structure) issues the license or has it issued by the Harry Fox Agency, and the album is released.

The record company feels "Doghouse Blues" has hit potential, so the song is released as a single. As the single begins to move up the charts, the publishing company's print department jumps into action and prints sheet music of "Doghouse Blues" with a photo of Spot and His 102 Dalmatians on the cover.

Meanwhile, the foreign department has notified the publishing company's sub-publishers that "Doghouse Blues" has been added to the catalog and that a recording of the song has been released in the United States. At this point each of the subpublishers' various departments will go into action just as the U.S. publisher did when the song was signed. If there are no plans for the American recording to be released in a particular subpublisher's territory, that subpublisher's creative department will go to work attempting to get a cover of "Doghouse Blues" (or an adaptation or translation of the song) for that territory.

Soon royalties are coming in to the publishing company from the record company, foreign sources and the performing rights society. Also, the print department reports to the royalty department on the amount of sheet music sold.

The royalty department then determines the amount of royalties due to Rover and Fido based on the contract each writer is bound by. Rover and Fido, of course, get their domestic and foreign performance royalties directly from the performing rights society but are paid their share of mechanical, print and other foreign royalties by the royalty department of the publishing company.

Now that the song is a hit, it's the job of the creative department and the licensing department to see to it that the song reaches its full potential. This means finding new uses for the song after it has run its course on the pop charts.

Commercials, movies and television shows are among the most obvious outlets for "Doghouse Blues" to continue to have a long, healthy life. Of course, overexposure can be dangerous to a copyright, so the publisher must be selective in determining which uses to allow and which to deny. All of us have grown extremely tired of songs to which we're continually subjected.

A great song that is not overexposed throughout the years can keep coming back to be a hit again and again. The classic song "Stand By Me" was a top twenty-five hit in 1961, 1967, 1970, 1975, 1980 and again in 1986. During that twenty-five-year period the song was used as the title and theme song of a movie and in no more than two or three commercials. If the publisher had chosen to allow every film, TV show and commercial request that came in over the years to be granted, we might all be pretty tired of the tune by now.

Granted, there aren't too many songs great enough to keep returning to the charts as "Stand By Me" has done, but a publisher who is careful about the manner in which a copyright is handled can actually earn millions of dollars during the time he owns and controls it.

Eight

STARTING YOUR OWN COMPANY

*M*usic publishing is a *business*. If you have a good head for business, you will want to seriously consider having your own publishing company at some point in your songwriting career.

Personally, it's hard for me to understand why a songwriter would want to give 100 percent of the publisher's share of his song to an outside publisher when some, most or even all of the publisher's share could belong to the songwriter's own publishing company.

However, I've almost always been on the business end of the music business, so I can't claim to know what it's like to actually be a professional songwriter and have a songwriter's point of view of music publishing. But I do know a lot of songwriters who have their own publishing companies, and I haven't met one yet who regretted the decision to step into the business world.

Since you've made it all the way to chapter eight of this book, it's apparent that you are interested enough in publishing that one day you will probably want to have your own publishing company—if not at the beginning of your career, then as soon as possible after the hits start coming.

The bottom line is this: If you write a song and allow me to be your publisher, I get half of all the royalties your song earns. If you allow me to copublish a song with your publishing company, and the publishing is split 50/50, then I get 25 percent of all the income your song makes. If you want me to administer your publishing company at a rate of 15 percent of the gross income, then I get 15 percent of all of the royalties.

If you have your own publishing company and you administer that company yourself, then I get nothing and you get 100 percent of the publisher's share and 100 percent of the songwriter's share. However, there is a lot of work involved in administering a publishing company and enough expenses that you may be better off allowing someone else to administer your company for you.

Unless your attitude is that you just don't want to be bothered with having to deal with business details at all, it seems logical that—at some point in your career—you should form your own publishing company, even if your songs are split with another publisher or if you decide to rely on outside administration. After all, a professional administrator or an administering copublisher will take

If you have your own publishing company and you administer that company yourself, you get 100 percent of the publisher's share and 100 percent of the songwriter's share.

care of most of the important publishing business for you, leaving you more time to write songs. And whatever the administrator's fee or copublisher's percentage may be, it certainly won't cost you as much as it would to sign all of the publishing away to an outside company.

I have known hundreds of songwriters and have met very few successful ones who didn't have a publishing company of their own. Granted, many of these songwriters' biggest hits were signed away to outside publishers early in their careers. It was usually this "live and learn" aspect of their lives that caused them eventually to start their own companies in the first place.

Rupert Holmes is one successful writer who determined that self-publishing was right for him. "I had a record deal and I was producing my own albums," he says. "I didn't know anyone who was going to do anything great for my songs that I couldn't do myself. It made more sense for me to keep the publishing until someone could show me that it made more sense for *them* to acquire the publishing. And the only time it made more sense was when a publisher offered to give me a great deal of money and split the publishing so that I got to keep half of it. For half of the publishing they would also do the administration, which was a lot of paperwork I didn't want to do myself."

If you are still doubtful about the importance of having your own company, find a successful songwriter who doesn't own or co-own the publishing on his biggest hit and ask him if he wishes he had the publishing on that song, or if he's happy about having it published by an outside company—particularly if that outside company now owns hundreds of thousands of other copyrights.

THE BIG "CATCH-22"

Seemingly, there is a major "catch-22" involved here. Almost all of us who applied for our very first job sat across the desk from a prospective employer who told us, "You can't get a job without some experience," to which we replied, "But how can I have had any experience if I haven't had a job before?"

Right now you might be thinking, "How can I have a publishing company if I don't have a song recorded? And if I'm going to have a song recorded, how is that possible without going to an outside publisher?"

As I said in chapter six, as a songwriter you always have options available to you. A couple of those major options are copublishing your song with an established publisher or allowing an outside publisher or independent administrator to administer your publishing company for you.

At the beginning of your songwriting career, it might be very difficult to get your first song cut by a major artist on a major label and still walk away with 100 percent of the publishing.

I'll be the first to admit that, at the beginning of your songwriting career, it might be very difficult to get your first song cut by a major artist on a major label and still walk away with 100 percent of the publishing. However, it's not impossible. If your song is good enough and an artist wants to record it badly enough, you're in a powerful position.

Should you—by some stroke of luck—reach that position, you might be tempted with a single song agreement offering a massive advance against future royalties, a staff writer deal, a copublishing agreement or a host of other wonderful things that might seem impossible to pass up.

But that big advance might actually turn out to be a loan of a sum of money that you would have been entitled to anyway should the song become a hit; you might not want to be tied down to a staff writer deal; and a copublishing agreement will still usually take away more than an administrator's fee would.

"But wait!" you say. "How did my song get into the hands of that major artist without a publisher?" The answer is: *You* would be the publisher. Acting as your own music publisher would cut out the middleman that many songwriters believe is an absolute requisite to becoming a successful songwriter.

Of course, I don't want to imply that going out and getting your own songs recorded by superstars (or anyone else) is a simple task. In fact, one of the main advantages of being signed to an established publishing company is having access to the creative department's contacts in the recording and film industries. I'm only trying to point out that, should you begin to develop contacts in those industries, you might find yourself in a position to plug your songs and not have to sign away part or all of the publishing.

THE SONGWRITER/PERFORMER

If you or your band sign a recording contract, it is almost essential that you have your own publishing company. Why sign a publishing agreement with the publishing company that's affiliated with the record company or with an outside publishing company if you are the one responsible for getting your songs recorded in the first place?

One of the main functions of a publisher is supposed to be to exploit your songs. If you are a recording artist, you are exploiting your own songs when you record them yourself. If your songs are signed to an outside publisher, you don't really want him to be trying to get your songs cut by other acts right away. If he does, you may find yourself competing against another act who's trying to get a hit with the same song you're trying to take up the charts. So, in this case, what's the point of having an outside publisher? Do you really need him to collect your money and keep part of it, when you've done all the legwork necessary to get the songs cut?

Even worse is the idea of signing a publishing agreement with the publishing company affiliated with the record company. The main function of a record company is to make and sell records. In many cases, their publishing company is merely collecting money from the record company across the hall (or across the room).

Along with the record company's affiliated publishing company, another modern problem that the songwriter/performer faces is something called the "controlled composition clause."

Rupert Holmes has some thoughts on this clause, which exists in many singer/ songwriters' recording contracts today. "I kind of loathe the era that we are in now where the record companies loom up and say, 'No more Mr. Nice Guy. We're going to have our cake and eat it, too.' One of the things that particularly offends me is that some record labels are saying that artists who are singing their own songs should get a lower royalty rate for their songs than outside songwriters. And yet, the very reason that the artist has been signed often will be because of the artistry of his songwriting—not the artistry of his voice."

Controlled compositions are songs owned and controlled by the songwriter/ performer. Generally this means songs written by the songwriter/performer and not signed to an outside publisher. A "controlled composition clause" in the recording

If you or your band sign a recording contract, it is almost essential that you have your own publishing company.

A *"controlled composition clause"* in the recording contract of a songwriter/ performer states that the record company will pay a reduced rate on the titles controlled by the artist.

contract of a songwriter/performer states that the record company will pay a reduced rate on the titles controlled by the artist.

This means that a song on the album written by an outside party will earn more for that party than a song written by the recording artist will earn the artist as a songwriter.

Even worse, there are some controlled composition clauses that allow the record company to pay a reduced mechanical rate on *all* of the songs in an album. In other words, if the clause says that the record company will pay 75 percent of statutory rate on all the songs that appear on the artist's album, the artist may have to take a cut in pay if any outside noncontrolled songs are included!

Here's how it would work: Joe is a singer/songwriter who has a controlled composition clause in his contract that says the record company will pay 75 percent of statutory for all of the songs on his album. Joe records five songs he wrote himself and five songs written by other songwriters. Unfortunately for Joe, the publishers of the five outside songs refuse to grant a reduced rate for the use of their songs.

The maximum amount the record company will agree to pay for the ten songs is 52⅛ cents per album (5.2125 cents times 10). Meanwhile, the outside publishers are demanding a total of 34¾ cents for their five songs (the statutory rate of 6.95 cents times 5). This means Joe is only going to receive 17.375 cents for his own five songs (52⅛ cents minus 34¾ cents)—the equivalent of only 3.475 cents per song. Although the songwriter/performer may find it difficult-to-impossible to achieve, it is in his best interest to attempt to have any proposed controlled composition clause language removed from his contract before signing with a record company.

To carry this concept another step, imagine an album of ten songs filled with sampled material. On top of the controlled composition clause which allows the artist to receive only 10 times the 75 percent of statutory rate, there are all the outside songs to be considered which were sampled in the first place. It is entirely conceivable that the sampled songs could use up all the mechanical royalties which the record company has granted to the artist, as well as cutting into the performer's artist royalties.

For example, let's say that an artist writes and records ten "new" songs, but samples twenty other songs over the course of those ten. (To try to keep this simple, we'll say that each of the artist's "new" songs include two samples of outside songs.) Then let's say that each of the publishers for those twenty outside songs demands that their share of the "new" songs the artist created (using samples of the outside publishers' songs) should receive 50 percent of the mechanical royalties. At this point, each of the artist's "new" songs now has a mechanical royalty of zero, since each of the outside publishers is demanding 50 percent. What happens if the twenty publishers in question each want to charge the statutory rate? The answer is, the outside publishers will jointly end up getting paid 69½ cents. Suddenly the artist is in the hole for 17.375 cents (69½ cents minus 52⅛ cents). Let's hope he's getting a good royalty as an artist, or this album is going to cost him money every time he sells a copy!

This might be an exaggeration, but only a slight one. Hopefully for the sake of the artist who samples extensively, the outside publishers won't ask for such high percentages of the songs that the sampler has created using those publishers' copyrights.

WHEN SHOULD YOU YIELD TO TEMPTATION?

By now I may have convinced you that self-publishing is something you should strongly consider. But in the music business there are very few absolutes. If self-publishing seems such an obvious route to take, why doesn't everyone start his own publishing company and publish 100 percent of everything he writes?

As I said at the beginning of this chapter, some songwriters may prefer not to deal with the "business" aspect of music publishing. This argument doesn't really hold water, though, because successful songwriting itself results in a great amount of business to be attended to. Unless you write for the sheer pleasure of writing, with no intention of having your songs recorded, a lot of nonsongwriting activities will be heaped upon you. For instance, you will need to learn how to read royalty statements. You will have to have an accountant and a lawyer. The accountant will require you to keep track of your expenses and receipts, while your lawyer will spend your time advising you about contracts and other legal details of the songwriting life. There is always much paperwork to do and much time to be consumed by things that aren't nearly as creative or enjoyable as songwriting itself.

Despite the fact that "business" is unavoidable, there are other strong reasons for going with an outside publisher. If a publisher hears your song and offers you a large advance, he is offering you something your own publishing company can't. This is where many songwriters decide to throw the concept of self-publishing out the window.

If a publisher tells you that Bruce Bighits is his best friend and that Bruce is in the studio right now, but Bruce will only record your song if the publisher delivers it to him by hand (and by the way, here's a five thousand dollar advance), and you've never had a song recorded by anybody before—you may find your hand has separated itself from the rest of your body and has signed on that dotted line without your being able to stop it.

Then there is the matter of the record deal. If you are a songwriter/performer and you have been turned down by several record companies, you might be offered a recording contract by a label if—and only if—you sign a publishing or copublishing agreement with the record company's publishing arm.

It's not always easy (and sometimes it might not even be wise) to insist on having 100 percent of the publishing on every song you write. Every case is different and depends on the situation and circumstances. One thing is certain, though. You don't want to give away the publishing if the occasion arises that you don't have to.

So, it's best to be ready for that moment when it appears that luck is on your side—when a record producer you know is in the studio and desperate for one more song, or when it turns out that the drunk guy you drove home from a bar last night is actually a major recording artist who now owes you his life and is looking for new songs for his next album.

Whatever the scenario, if you can keep some or all of the publishing in a particular situation, you should be prepared to do so, if not by already having your own company, then at least by having the knowledge necessary to set up a publishing company when that proper moment arrives.

So if I'm so gung-ho about self-publishing, why have I written the first seven chapters of this book? One reason is fairly obvious: Most songwriters (especially

It's not always easy (and sometimes it might not even be wise) to insist on having 100 percent of the publishing on every song you write. Every case is different and depends on the situation and circumstances.

the nonperforming type) are probably going to find themselves having to deal with outside publishers for some time as a means of achieving success. A staff writer earning a thousand dollars or more a week as an advance against future royalties can live comfortably with a feeling of security. Also, if you find yourself in an "offer too good to refuse" situation, you should know—from what you've learned in this book up to now—what some of the available options are.

Another reason for everything I've written so far is to give you the kind of knowledge that I hope will be of help to you if you set up your own company. The information that follows in this chapter should provide a starting point for you to learn how to form and run your own company. I have even tried to give you some pointers on some of the aspects of handling your own administration if you should be so inclined.

SETTING UP SHOP

Becoming a music publisher doesn't have to be terribly difficult or expensive. Unlike businesses that require the actual manufacturing of a product, music publishing is largely a business of intangibles. Like all businesses, your publishing company has to exist somewhere. I would recommend that you begin with that basic tool of most small businesses—the kitchen table. If you're lucky enough to have a spare room in your house or apartment, that's a fine workstation too.

There are generally three business structures in this country: the sole proprietorship, the partnership and the corporation. Once you have made the decision to form your own publishing company, you will want to speak with a lawyer and/or an accountant about which of these three types of business arrangements makes the most sense for you from a legal and financial standpoint.

The most common of these three enterprises for the small business is the sole proprietorship. Since you will probably want to start your company on a small scale, the sole proprietorship is usually the best avenue to take. However, everyone's financial circumstances are different, so you really should speak to an attorney or an accountant you trust so that they can let you know if your financial status would make forming a partnership or a corporation more feasible for you.

To set up a sole proprietorship, in most parts of the country it is necessary to file a DBA form at your city hall or county courthouse. DBA stands for "Doing Business As." You can find standard DBA forms at almost any stationery store.

One of the purposes of filing a DBA form is to officially inform your local government of the name of your business venture. Coming up with a name for your publishing company is an important step in becoming a publisher.

It is at this juncture that you will have to decide which performing rights society your company is going to be affiliated with. If you are already affiliated with a society as a songwriter, that is the society your own publishing company will have to be affiliated with as well.

Assuming you are not already affiliated with a performing rights society as a songwriter, deciding which society you will want to affiliate with as a writer and self-publisher should not be a lighthearted choice on your part. You've already read about all three organizations in chapter four of this book. If you haven't already made contact with any of the societies at this point in your career, now is the time.

Write or call all three societies (ASCAP, BMI and SESAC), and ask them to

Unlike businesses that require the actual manufacturing of a product, music publishing is largely a business of intangibles.

You will have to decide which performing rights society your company is going to be affiliated with.

send you information about their organizations, as well as an application for writer and publisher membership. Read the literature, then talk to others you may know who are affiliated songwriters or publishers and get their opinions on the particular societies they belong to.

I would also strongly urge you to talk to representatives of each society on the phone. Are they friendly? Are they helpful? Do they sound like they're interested in having you affiliated with them? Once you've done your preliminary research, call them all back again. Can you get them on the phone? If not, do they return your call promptly?

The reason I'm putting an emphasis on this aspect of your business is that your performance royalty income is very important. If you have questions about whether or not you are being paid properly by your performing rights society, you don't want to have to wait days, weeks or months for an answer.

Having been the manager of several publishing companies, I have dealt with both BMI and ASCAP frequently. Some of the companies I have run have had several hundred songwriters signed to them, and on more than one occasion I've discovered that a songwriter with the same name as one of my writers was getting money that was supposed to be going to mine. I've also had cases where the songwriters' percentages (in the case of songs that have two or more writers) were being split improperly.

On the publishing end I've dealt with situations where royalties due for a song that had been transferred to one of my publishing companies were still being paid to the previous publisher. The number of things that can go wrong in the publishing business is almost unbelievable.

I discovered a long time ago that the only way to get these problems corrected was to make contacts at the societies and hound them if necessary until things got fixed. Since you will be starting from scratch and operating on a small level at the beginning, you're not as likely to encounter the same kind of problems as would a publisher with thousands of copyrights. However, it's good to make those initial contacts and find out who you think you will be best able to work with before you lock yourself into a society for an extended period of time.

Once you have decided which society is good enough (and fortunate enough) to be the performing rights society for you and your publishing company, you will have to fill out the songwriter and publisher affiliation applications. It is at this point that you will have to pick a name for your company, plus a couple of options in case the name you've chosen is already in use or is too similar to another publishing company's name.

The performing rights society will check the names of all other existing publishing companies and will inform you which of your name choices is available. If you have come up with a particular name for your company that you're anxious to have, you might want to call your contact at the performing rights society you've chosen and see if that name is available even before you fill out the publisher affiliation application. If it is, you should ask them to reserve the name for you.

Remember that your company name is going to represent you, so choose something that is appropriate and that will look good on your stationery, business cards, and in small type on CDs and cassettes.

Once your name has been approved, it's time to fill out your DBA form and file your business name in the manner required by your local government.

Remember that your company name is going to represent you, so choose something that is appropriate and that will look good on your stationery, business cards and in small type on CDs and cassettes.

You should also check with your bank to find out what information they require for your business checking account. Once you have a name, a bank account in your company name and a performing rights society affiliation, you're officially in business. If your state or county requires more on your part (especially in the area of business taxes), your accountant or lawyer should be able to provide you with that information.

THE COMPANY IMAGE

As a music publisher, your company will need to have a professional image. Since much of your business will involve correspondence, your stationery should complement that image. A sheet of plain white paper won't do.

You might want to start by looking at the stationery of other publishing companies. If you've sent tapes out and have gotten rejection letters back (and if you didn't throw them out in a fit of anger), take a look at them now.

Most publishers' stationery that I've seen looks pretty conservative. If most of your songs are novelty tunes, you might want to have stationery that reflects that image. Just keep in mind that your stationery and business cards are representing you and the songs in your publishing company, as is your company name.

The information on your letterhead should consist of your company name, address, phone number, and—in case you have a few bucks to spare—your fax machine number. All of the major music publishers now have fax machines. Since my company has had one for many years, it's hard to remember how I functioned without it. However, it must not be absolutely essential, because we all survived without one until recently. Besides, they can be expensive, and you don't want to go overboard on a venture that will require a lot of work and luck to succeed.

YOUR MUSIC PUBLISHING OFFICE

By day I currently work in a large office with a high-backed black leather chair, a dramatic glass-top desk, gold and platinum albums on one wall, original artwork on another, and a handmade wall unit that holds all of my audio equipment. The wall behind my desk is a giant window that faces the Hollywood Hills. Outside my office is a large waiting room where a receptionist sits, keeping an eye on who's coming in and going out all day.

The office is on Sunset Boulevard in Los Angeles, in the heart of the music industry of that city. Overall, it's a pretty impressive setup.

By night, however, if I'm not out attending one of the many music industry functions that take place pretty frequently in this town, I work in a spare room in my house, using a former dining room table as my desk. There are no gold records or expensive paintings in this room. Since writers don't have frequent visitors coming to their places of business, I'm not out to impress anyone with my work space.

As a self-publisher, you don't need to try to impress anyone with a fancy office. You are running a small home business that should remain small until enough money comes rolling in to justify those other accoutrements that come with a large, successful enterprise.

As a self-publisher, you don't need to try to impress anyone with a fancy office. Most of your work will be done on the phone, via the fax machine, through the mail or in person. But rather than people coming to see you, you'll be going to them. Always keep in mind that you are running a small home business that should remain small until enough money comes rolling in to someday justify an actual office with a secretary, a high-backed leather chair and all of those other accoutrements that come with a large, successful enterprise.

So what will your home office need and how much expense will be involved? Since you're a songwriter, you probably already have much of what you need. If you've been sending your songs out to publishers, then you've been printing copies of your lyrics, either via typewriter or computer.

A typewriter is okay, but if you are a part of the computer generation and have your own home computer, then that's even better. As I said earlier about fax machines, though, major publishers operated for decades without computers, so if a typewriter is all you have, it will certainly be sufficient for a small operation, at least until the expense of a computer is justifiable.

Two more items essential to your operation are a telephone and an answering machine. Along with your written correspondence, your phone is your contact to the outside world.

You will need an answering machine because you can't possibly be where your phone is at all times. Most likely you have school or a day job that will keep you away from your phone when important calls are coming in. You might want to get the kind of answering machine from which you can retrieve messages by calling it from another location.

One other thought about answering machines: Make your machine's message as brief and professional-sounding as you can. If someone is taking the time to call your place of business, they don't want to sit through bad jokes, thirty seconds of your latest composition or anything else that distracts from the reason they are calling you.

The only exception to this advice is if your image is off-the-wall in the first place. If all you write are hilarious novelty tunes, feel free to have a field day with your answering machine. If you deal only in serious ballads, my advice is to stick to the basics.

I realize this may seem like a small point to dwell on, but more than one person has missed out on a serious opportunity when I hung up on thirty seconds of gibberish coming from an answering machine that I didn't have time to listen to.

Your remaining major purchases—tape recorders—might already be in your home since you're a songwriter. If you have your own home recording studio and a good quality cassette machine, you've got everything you need in the way of recording equipment—at least until technology makes your equipment outdated. If you've been making all of your demo tapes at a recording studio and having your cassettes dubbed by a tape duplication service, you might find things to be more cost effective if you purchase some tape dubbing equipment of your own.

When you are beginning a small publishing company, you have to keep in mind that professional-sounding demos are very important. There are professional publishers all around you using the latest technologies available. When I speak at songwriting seminars and workshops, I always remind those in attendance that they are not only competing against the other songwriters at their level, they are also competing against the person who wrote the song sitting at the top of the *Billboard* chart this week.

The same thought applies to you as a publisher. You're in competition with Warner/Chappell Music, EMI, MCA Music, Sony Music, PolyGram and every other major and minor publisher in the business today. You're even in competition with me! So, even if your publishing empire is in one corner of your bedroom, you have

As a publisher, you're in competition with every other major and minor publisher in the business today.

to give the outward appearance of being a professional enterprise.

When it comes to your demos, you'll need to have the facilities to make the best tapes possible. This means being able to transfer your finished demo from the master tape onto the tape you'll want to present with as little loss in sound quality as possible.

Since technology changes frequently, I can't presume to know what will be in demand in the years ahead. For the last few years the standard device for song presentations has been the cassette tape. When I send a cassette to a producer, I make sure that it's as close to the quality of the original recording as I can get it.

One more essential item for your publishing company is a subscription to *Billboard*, the most popular trade journal in the music business. The subscription rate is pretty high, so be prepared to lay out some serious money. If you have a songwriting partner or a friend who's in need of a subscription as well, maybe the two of you can subscribe to it together. *Billboard* will provide you with the type of information you will need to know to make contacts, see what acts are on the charts, find out the latest changes in the publishing business and lots of other important news.

Before we get into the business of operating a small-scale publishing company, let's review everything you're going to need to get started. First, you'll require a space to operate in. In the beginning that space can be the size of a kitchen table or a desk.

Next you'll need to find out what type of business structure is best for you: a sole proprietorship, a partnership, or a corporation.

Then you will need to create a name for your company (with a couple of options in case your first choice is already taken). Once you have chosen your name(s), you will need to apply for affiliation with the performing rights society that you have decided upon—a decision you shouldn't make until you've done your own research and have found the society that works best for you.

Once your name has been approved and you have filed the proper documents required by your local government, you will need to create (or have someone else create) your company's professional look via stationery and business cards.

For correspondence and generally keeping track of your operation, you will need a typewriter or, better yet, a personal computer. You will also need a phone and an answering machine. If possible, a fax machine may prove to be a wise investment.

You will need high quality equipment for making demos and copies of your demos. The songs on your demos are the product that your business is manufacturing and selling. I know that sounds impersonal, but it is the ultimate reality of music publishing. Therefore, your product must be excellent to compete with the other publishers who are trying to market their product to the same buyers you are trying to reach.

Finally, you'll need a subscription to *Billboard*, the trade journal that will keep you abreast of everything that's happening in the music business.

DAY-TO-DAY OPERATION

Now that you're in business, it's time to cover what you will need to do and who you'll need to get to know to make your operation survive and grow.

As a self-publisher, you must either have an administrator (which may not be necessary until you get a song recorded and released) or you must handle all of

As a self-publisher, you must handle all of the departments and functions of a full-scale publishing company yourself.

the departments and functions of a full-scale publishing company yourself. Since your main effort is to get your songs recorded and released, your primary function is to act as the creative manager of your company.

This means making contacts in the music industry and choosing which of your songs to send to which contacts. If you live in or near one of the major music centers (New York City, Nashville, Los Angeles, etc.), the time has come to start shoving your foot in the door by meeting artists' managers, record producers, recording artists, A&R men and women, agents and anyone else who might be able to help you.

Everyone's experience in acquiring contacts is different, making it very difficult for anyone to say, "Here's the proper way to get to know people in the music business." My personal method was so strange that it would be almost impossible for anyone to duplicate.

The short version goes like this: I got on a bus in Florence, Alabama, rode to New York City, and began looking for a job. My first job was as an assistant to the general manager of a well-known print publishing firm. After about a year with no movement upward in the company, I got a job in a museum called the Songwriters Hall of Fame where I met some of the top songwriters in the business.

Not long after I went to work there, the gentleman who had hired me left the organization. Since I had been his assistant, the board of directors promoted me to his position.

Among other things, it was my job to coordinate the annual awards dinners. One of the board members who showed some personal interest in me told me it was important to get to know everyone I could if I wanted to move up in the music business. At the annual awards dinners I met an amazing array of the biggest names in the entertainment world.

As fate would have it, we lost our lease on the space where the museum was housed. When we were offered space for a small office in a building on West Fifty-seventh Street in Manhattan, I ended up working on the same floor with a record company.

As you might have guessed, I went to work for the record company, eventually running its affiliated publishing company. Meanwhile, I was elected to the board of directors of the Songwriters Hall of Fame, which allowed me to continue to meet more and more people in the industry at each function the Hall of Fame held.

Always realizing the importance of keeping my name and face in the public eye, I made friends with the trade press who attended the same functions I was attending. I also made friends with a photographer who I made sure was standing nearby with camera in hand when I was chatting with Willie Nelson, Chuck Berry, Eubie Blake, Henry Mancini, Carole King, Ed Koch (the former Mayor of New York City), Dick Clark and others.

With a minimal amount of begging I managed to get my photos with some of these famous people in such trade papers as *Billboard* and *Cashbox*, as well as newspapers and the occasional magazine. Since many of the people I needed to know in the music business were subscribers to the music trades, I managed to become a semifamiliar name and face to them.

Granted, I'm not as well known as the presidents of the major record companies (or even the vice presidents, for that matter), but I have made enough contacts over the years that I can get the attention of almost anyone I need to speak to or get a tape to. If I don't know the record producer of a hot act I have a song for, it's almost a sure thing that I know someone who does. With a little networking, I will get my tape heard.

As you can see from my own story, there is no set way to get to know the people you need to know. However, it's not impossible, because new songwriters and publishers are managing to get their songs cut all the time.

Acting as the creative manager of your publishing company, you will have to learn to hustle. In case you're thinking that you'd rather not be your own publisher if it means having to be brave enough to go out and meet high-powered music executives, let me remind you that it takes an awful lot of work and effort to go out and meet music publishers. If your songs are going to be heard, you're going to have to start making contacts sooner or later.

But the question remains, "How do I meet these seemingly elusive music industry types?" To me, the most obvious method is to attend the various workshops and seminars that music executives are always speaking at.

In the major cities like New York, Nashville and Los Angeles, there are seminars going on all the time that are sponsored by ASCAP, BMI, the National Academy of Popular Music, the Songwriters Guild of America and other music organizations. Get on the phone, call these organizations,* and find out when and where their next function is taking place. Some seminars are free; others have fees attached. Much like the Copyright Act, tax laws are always changing, but as a publisher, you will probably be able to write off these types of fees as business expenses.

If you're lucky at these seminars, you might learn something about the business that you don't already know. The main reason for being there, though, is to meet the speakers who can do you some good, as well as any music executives who might be in attendance.

Don't go to these functions unprepared. This is where your subscription to *Billboard* is worth its annual rate. Once you're signed up to attend a specific seminar and you know who the speakers will be, check through your issues of *Billboard* to see if you can get some detailed information about what these speakers have accomplished lately. Does that record producer have a big hit on the charts? Did that A&R person just get a big promotion? Did that manager just sign a performer who uses outside material and sings the kind of songs you write? Get to know these people before you ever meet them in person.

PUTTING IT ALL TOGETHER

If your songs are good, if you make enough contacts, if you refuse to give up, and if luck is on your side, then the day will finally come when someone somewhere records one of your songs. At that point, as a self-publisher you will either need to apply the information you've learned from this book regarding the way a publishing company operates or allow an outside administrator to do the detail work for you (and monitor their work based on all you now know).

If you get a song in your publishing company recorded, then you have fulfilled your initial duties as a creative manager. Next, if you should decide to try your

---

*The addresses and phone numbers of some of these organizations are listed in the Appendix.

hand at administration, you will have to put on your licensing department hat.

The party releasing the initial recording of your song will require a mechanical license from you. Since this is the first recording of a particular work, the copyright law says you have the right to determine whether you want this first recording to be made and distributed, as well as the right to determine the royalty rate.

Realistically, though, unless the initial recording is so bad that you want to prevent its release, you are obviously going to give permission. Also, you wouldn't want to charge more than the current statutory mechanical rate. (Although it is allowed by law, I'm not aware of anyone who has actually charged more than statutory.) You may even find yourself having to grant a reduced rate if circumstances require it. In fact, the label releasing the initial recording of your song may have agreed to do so only if you agreed to grant a three-quarter rate.

But to issue a mechanical license, you need to know how the license should read. One example of a mechanical license can be found in the Appendix. If you prefer to have your licensing handled through the Harry Fox Agency, this would be the time to contact them about representing you in this area.

Whether you issue licenses yourself or whether you use the Fox Agency, your publishing company will be carrying out another duty required to bring you closer to actually earning royalties.

When royalties are due from the record company that has released a recording of your song, you will need to keep track of the royalties you receive. If your mechanical license calls for royalty payments to be due within forty-five days of each calendar quarter, you will probably get paid very close to or on the forty-fifth day.

One of the primary ways money is made by record companies is from the interest earned on the vast amounts of money held by the record company prior to making payments to artists and publishers. Record companies have historically taken full advantage of this "forty-five-day" clause, so there's no real reason to expect monies due to you to show up any earlier than the record company is contractually obligated to send them.

Once the forty-five days are up, however, you should receive royalties on records made and distributed during the quarter in question. Assuming payment is made (and reputable record companies will usually pay on time), it's your job as the royalty department of your publishing company to make sure the amount of money received is the number of copies reported on the statement times the mechanical rate agreed to in your mechanical license. If it is, congratulations. If it's not, it's time for you to get on the phone and contact the royalty department of the record company. If there is a discrepancy, it's your responsibility to get it corrected.

Unless you happen to be a combination publisher/lawyer, though, you can't be your own legal department. If you find yourself in a situation where a record company refuses to pay you at all within the prescribed time period or thirty or more days thereafter, you most likely have grounds for a breach of contract suit. If the breach is determined by the court to be material, you would then claim that the agreement is terminated and that further acts of manufacture and distribution constitute copyright infringement.

However, before you start spending legal fees, it's best to decide if the money you're not being paid by the record company is substantially more than the amount of money your lawyer is going to charge to recover it. If the answer is no, make your best effort to recover the money yourself by hounding the record company and threatening legal action. Another angle would be to use a lawyer willing to work on a contingency basis, in which case the lawyer's fee would be a percentage of the money recovered.

Once "distribution of phonorecords . . . to the public by sale" has taken place, your composition qualifies as having been published. As your own copyright department, you will need to inform your performing rights society that your song has been released on record so that the society will be able to properly account to you.

If your song is a hit, it's likely that you will be approached by print publishers for the right to release your song in sheet music and folio form. Although you will probably be able to negotiate the basic points of the agreement (amount of advance, royalty per copy, etc.), you will need a lawyer to look over the agreement to make suggestions or implement changes he feels are necessary.

Since the recording of your song will probably be released in foreign territories, you will need to start making subpublishing deals. Acting as your own foreign department, this will mean deciding which of the options discussed in chapter five are best for your company. Obviously you won't want to go around setting up your own foreign corporations, but you will need to get involved with subpublishers on some level since there is the potential of serious money to be made in the foreign market.

This is the point at which you'll find out the advantages of owning a fax machine. You will probably prefer not to do business in the middle of the night. While you're sleeping, your subpublisher in another time zone halfway around the world can be faxing you information about what is happening with your song there.

A hit song often prompts other types of uses, as I have pointed out in other sections of this book. It is possible you'll be getting calls requesting to use the song in commercials, movies or TV shows. In these situations you will have to once again don your licensing department hat to negotiate a fair price for these kinds of uses.

As a self-publisher, at one time or another you will have to be your own creative department. You will have to act as the licensing, royalty, copyright and foreign departments as well. The legal and print departments will be handled out-of-house by others qualified in those areas.

As a self-publisher, then, at one time or another you will at least have to be your own creative department. If you decide to delve into administration, you will have to act as the licensing, royalty, copyright and foreign departments as well. The legal and print departments, of course, will be handled out-of-house by others qualified in those areas.

As more of your songs are recorded, your publishing company may one day find it needs a real office with a part- or fulltime secretary. If your success rate becomes good enough, you may find yourself turning into a larger publishing company, taking on additional writers and bringing in large sums of money.

On the other hand, this can frequently lead to a situation where you find yourself buried in business details with little time for the more creative endeavors of being a songwriter.

You can either try to keep the company small enough for you to handle (most likely by using an outside administrator) or hire someone to act as an in-house administrator. Should you decide hire personnel, the important thing is to make sure that your company is active enough and financially successful enough to justify such expenses.

Nine

THE FUTURE OF MUSIC PUBLISHING

*A*ttempting to predict the future is not always a wise move—especially in print. Before I endeavor to prognosticate on things to come, let's take a look back at what I hope you have learned so far from this guide to music publishing.

Music publishing is an evolving industry. From the industry's earliest days in this country, publishers have been forced to keep up with musical, social and technological changes. Before the days of recordings and performance royalties, publishers reaped their profits from the printing and selling of sheet music and song books.

When records caught on with the public, publishers were in constant demand since performers and record companies were in need of new songs. The advent of motion pictures with sound also called for more songs to be created. Meanwhile, the first performing rights society in the United States had been formed, allowing publishers and songwriters a new avenue by which to earn royalties for their works.

As years went by, times changed, and artists began to record their own material; the publishing companies found themselves banging on the record companies' doors, with each publisher trying to sell record company executives on the idea that their songs were better than their competitors'. As the number of artists recording outside material grew ever smaller, competition among publishers grew stronger.

Eventually music publishers got into the business of artist development, selling the artist/songwriter package to record companies rather than just trying to convince a record company A&R person of the merits of one particular song.

Although the buying and selling of publishing catalogs is nothing new, beginning in the 1980s a sort of merger fever swept through the publishing industry. As one large company devoured another, the number of major publishers shrank to only a handful, making the resultant megapublishers cumbersome while allowing smaller publishers to prosper and grow at a more realistic rate.

As you learned in chapter two, the U.S. Copyright Act is the backbone of the music publishing business. Like publishing, it too has evolved with the advance of technology and creative expansion and diversification—although not as quickly as some might have wished.

Over the years, the life span of a copyright has increased dramatically; the addition of the right to royalties for public performance has, in some cases, doubled the amount of income available to many owners of active copyrights; and by joining the Berne Convention, U.S. copyright law is on close-to-equal footing with most of the countries throughout the rest of the world. Once the concept of "life plus seventy" is added in the U.S., our copyright law will be among the most protective in existence for those involved in the business of intellectual properties.

You have learned how publishers and songwriters can earn income from a song: through mechanical, synchronization, "new media," performance and print royalties, as well as royalties earned from foreign countries via subpublishing.

We have covered the main options available to you as a songwriter by discussing the various types of contracts publishers usually offer (single song, exclusive or staff writer, copublishing and adminstration), including some of the main clauses included in such contracts. By this time you no doubt realize the importance of having a good entertainment lawyer when any of these types of agreements are offered to you.

Next we went inside a music publishing company to discover how it functions. Although the legal, print and accounting divisions are frequently not part of the publisher's in-house operation, a workable company must consist of creative, licensing, royalty, copyright and foreign departments. Depending on the company's size, these departments may be handled by a small staff or by scores of employees around the world.

I have also shown you how it is possible to start your own music publishing company on a tight budget by operating out of your own home, handling most of the publishing company departments by yourself.

It took me many years of trial and error to learn what I have written on these pages. However, although I've saved you from almost two decades of study at the proverbial School of Hard Knocks, there will be much more for you to learn in the future—especially with the rapid growth going on in the world of technology. After all, you can't learn how to race in the Indianapolis 500 just by reading a driver's manual. You have to slowly gain skill and knowledge, and then put those traits to the test by applying what you've learned in here to the music publishing race going on out there.

THE FUTURE

When Columbia and RCA Records introduced versions of fine-grooved records that rotated at 33⅓ and 45 revolutions per minute, many people argued that the discs wouldn't become commercially acceptable since the general public would be required to pay higher prices for the records and to purchase new equipment to play them on.

Despite the fact that 78 rpm records quickly became passé after the introduction of these two new forms of vinyl records, "experts" more recently challenged the commercial viability of compact discs based on the same argument that the general public wouldn't be open to the idea of purchasing new audio equipment or paying substantially more money for CDs than they had been paying for LPs. To paraphrase Santayana, those who aren't aware of earlier goofy predictions are doomed to repeat them.

Of course, not every technological move the music industry made was an ongoing hit with the public. Although the 8-track tape was popular for a season, it was quickly replaced by the prerecorded cassette. This swift change by the general public was a sure sign that American society will not hesitate to move to a more practical, better quality product when it is introduced and properly marketed.

In the first edition of this book I said, "In the future the music industry will continue to create new types of phonorecords. If these devices are more practical and of higher audio quality than those then available in the marketplace, the current model will be replaced in a briefer period of time than the 'experts' will predict."

As I write this revised version of the book some seven years later, I have seen the quick rise and decline of the prerecorded Digital Audiotape. Who knows whether it will survive at all? Maybe it qualified as being "of higher audio quality" than CDs (or maybe not), but for the time being, it appears to have fallen far short of what most consumers consider to be "more practical." Perhaps its poor sales figures can be chalked up to something as simple as the public's impression that audiotape can be broken, whereas CDs seem to be less destructible.

On the other hand, there has been an interesting influx of new technology such as enhanced CDs, which have music on them just as regular CDs do, but which also include other material that can be viewed on one's computer or TV screen via a CD-ROM or DVD player. This additional material, of course, makes the enhanced CD more than just a phonorecord, since it also includes images.

With the incredible advancement of technology, I feel certain that new types of phonorecords will make the older types obsolete as long as they're more practical and of higher audio quality.

Also in the first edition of this book, I wrote: "I believe we are not too far away from a time when the industry will become tied into the personal computer. Although it may be a few years away, we will probably find ourselves with the capability of creating our own personalized compilation tapes. . . . In the future, a person will be able to enter his selections on his home computer and create a tape that contains the recordings of his choice."

There are now companies on the Internet which allow you to download recordings from their site for a fee, giving you "the capability of creating your own personalized compilation tapes." Those companies then pay mechanical royalties to the mechanical licensing organization in their country, which in turn pays the publishers of the songs that have been downloaded by the consumer.

I'm not trying to imply that record stores won't continue to exist in some form. However, it is interesting to note that, since the advent of television—and especially since the recent popularity of the Internet—American society has shown a pattern of spending more and more time at home. Also, by providing recorded music directly to the consumer, record companies now have the capacity to bypass the middlemen (in this case, distributors and and record stores) and make higher profits for themselves. There is no safer prediction than to say that, if a record company finds a method to make higher profits, that method will be implemented with great speed.

Before we delve too far into the futuristic possibilities of technology, let's consider music publishing's role in the immediate years ahead. Obviously, no matter what device is used to transmit recorded music, as long as the copyright law manages to keep up with technological advances and inflation, music publishers will continue to thrive. The big question is what form will publishing take in the future?

As I have said several times, the most radical change of recent vintage in the publishing world has been the remarkable number of mergers between the major players in the industry. When I first came up with the idea of writing this book, Warner Communications had not yet bought Chappell & Co. Shortly after I began working on the first edition, EMI bought SBK. Then, even before I had a chance to finish this new edition, Sony and ATV merged. In the first edition of this book, I predicted that "these mergers and takeovers will continue until there are only two or three major publishing companies in the country." I think we have reached a point where there are now only a handful of major players: Warner/Chappell, EMI, MCA, Sony/ATV, BMG and PolyGram.

I also predicted that these mergers—although financially profitable to the seller in the short term—would cause the industry to become very top-heavy, opening doors for dozens of smaller independent companies to compete on a more active basis. I think this, too, has come to fruition, since companies such as Windswept/Pacific, Rondor and Leiber & Stoller Music have become extremely successful in recent years, even though the size of their catalogs can't begin to compete with a company like Warner/Chappell.

When the record industry became a game with only a handful of major players, it was very difficult for independent labels to compete for space on the charts. Publishing differs, though, since songs are required by all record labels, large and small. Also, since an independent publishing company can exist with a very low overhead, it is an easier business to finance than an independent record company.

The biggest problem these large conglomerate-type publishers now find themselves facing is a lack of personal contact with the thousands and thousands of songwriters whose songs are signed to these megacompanies. Although smaller publishers may not be able to compete in the area of advances to staff writers, these smaller companies will be able to have a more personal relationship with their writers.

Back in 1989, Rupert Holmes saw the future this way: "The good news is that the music business will be making more money than ever. The bad news is that there will be fewer people making that money."

However, as Rupert predicted, for some there are advantages to the big business syndrome. "Anytime anything gets this huge and conglomerated, there are cracks in the hull of the huge corporate ship. That's where the smaller publisher is going to actually be in better shape than he was before. It's going to take smaller publishers who are willing to stick their necks out a little to make things really happen."

All these years later, it turns out that Rupert was exactly right. Maybe he and I should start one of those psychic hotlines! While the major publishing companies all seem to be run by lawyers and accountants these days, the smaller companies are mainly being run by real music men and women who got into the business to promote music rather than to constantly worry about numbers and legalese. Like crumbs from the king's table, many opportunities will continue to fall through the cracks of the major publishing companies' operations, and the smaller publishers will be there to pick them up and profit from them.

I predict that in the future there will be vast new opportunities for music publishers of all sizes. Not only will new technology cause improved products for publishers to profit from; there will also be new avenues for publishers to take to further exploit their songs.

Finally, I truly hope that the songwriting and publishing communities will gain more power politically, effecting more improvements in the area of copyright protection. This political clout will be a necessity if the publishing industry wishes to prevent the loss of untold millions of dollars through illegal copying—a process that will become easier and easier with the advent of new technology unless laws are created to curtail the practice.

TO YOUR FUTURE

Musical fads will come and go, but there will always be a demand for good songs. As a songwriter, determining where you're going to fit into this constantly changing industry will be up to you, your talent and a heaping dose of luck.

Now that you know what music publishing is and how it functions, it's time to act on your newfound knowledge. If you keep up with the changes in the business, keep having faith in yourself, and keep your fingers crossed, you will succeed. Remember, thousands upon thousands of others have done it. So can you. Here's to your future!

Appendix

U.S. PERFORMING RIGHTS SOCIETIES AND SOME MAJOR SONGWRITERS' AND PUBLISHERS' ORGANIZATIONS

American Society of Composers, Authors and Publishers (ASCAP)*
    One Lincoln Plaza, New York, NY 10023; (212) 621-6000
    7920 Sunset Blvd., Suite 300, Los Angeles, CA 90046; (213) 883-1000
    2 Music Square West, Nashville, TN 37203; (615) 742-5000

Association of Independent Music Publishers (AIMP)
    120 E. 56th St., Suite 1150, New York, NY 10022; (212) 758-6157
    P.O. Box 1561, Burbank, CA 91507; (818) 842-6257

Broadcast Music, Inc. (BMI)*
    320 W. 57th St., New York, NY 10019; (212) 586-2000
    10 Music Square East, Nashville, TN 37203; (615) 401-2000
    8730 Sunset Blvd., 3rd Floor West, Los Angeles, CA 90069; (310) 659-9109

California Copyright Conference (CCC)
    P.O. Box 1291, Burbank, CA 91507; (818) 848-6783

Nashville Songwriters Association, International (NSAI)
    15 Music Square West, Nashville, TN 37203; (615) 256-3354

National Academy of Popular Music—Songwriters' Hall of Fame
    330 W. 58th St., Suite 411, New York, NY 10019-1827; (212) 957-9230

National Academy of Songwriters (NAS)
    6381 Hollywood Blvd., Suite 780, Hollywood, CA 90028; (213) 463-7178

National Music Publishers Association (NMPA)
    711 Third Ave., New York, NY 10017; (212) 370-5330

SESAC, Inc.*
    55 Music Square East, Nashville, TN 37203; (615) 320-0055
    421 W. 54th St., New York, NY 10019; (212) 586-3450

Songwriters Guild of America (SGA)
    1500 Harbor Blvd., Weehawken, NJ 07087-6732; (201) 867-7603
    6430 Sunset Blvd., Hollywood, CA 90028; (213) 462-1108
    1222 16th Ave. South, Suite 25, Nashville, TN 37212; (615) 329-1782

*Performing Rights Societies

The Songwriters Guild of America

NOTE TO SONGWRITERS: (A) DO NOT SIGN THIS CONTRACT IF IT HAS ANY CHANGES UNLESS YOU HAVE FIRST DISCUSSED SUCH CHANGES WITH THE GUILD; (B) FOR YOUR PROTECTION PLEASE SEND A FULLY EXECUTED COPY OF THIS CONTRACT TO THE GUILD.

POPULAR SONGWRITERS CONTRACT
© Copyright 1978 AGAC

AGREEMENT made this   day of   , 19   , between

....

(hereinafter called "Publisher") and ....

....

(Jointly and/or severally hereinafter collectively called "Writer");

WITNESSETH:

Composition
(Insert title
of composition→
here)

1. The Writer hereby assigns, transfers and delivers to the Publisher a certain heretofore unpublished original musical composition, written and/or composed by the above-named Writer now entitled ....
.... (hereinafter referred to as "the composition"), including the title, words and music thereof, and the right to secure copyright therein throughout the entire world, and to have and to hold the said copyright and all rights of whatsoever nature thereunder existing, for

(Insert number→
of years here)

.... years from the date of this contract or 35 years from the date of the first release of a *not more than 40* commercial sound recording of the composition, whichever term ends earlier, unless this contract is sooner terminated in accordance with the provisions hereof.

Performing
Rights Affiliation

2. In all respects this contract shall be subject to any existing agreements between the parties hereto and the following small performing rights licensing organization with which Writer and Publisher are affiliated:

(Delete Two) ⟶ (ASCAP, BMI, SESAC). Nothing contained herein shall, or shall be deemed to, alter, vary or modify the rights of Writer and Publisher to share in, receive and retain the proceeds distributed to them by such small performing rights licensing organization pursuant to their respective agreement with it.

Warranty

3. The Writer hereby warrants that the composition is his sole, exclusive and original work, that he has full right and power to make this contract, and that there exists no adverse claim to or in the composition, except as aforesaid in Paragraph 2 hereof and except such rights as are specifically set forth in Paragraph 23 hereof.

Royalties
(Insert amount
of advance here) ⟶

4. In consideration of this contract, the Publisher agrees to pay the Writer as follows:

(a) $..................... as an advance against royalties, receipt of which is hereby acknowledged, which sum shall remain the property of the Writer and shall be deductible only from payments hereafter becoming due the Writer under this contract.

Piano Copies

(b) In respect of regular piano copies sold and paid for in the United States and Canada, the following royalties per copy:

Sliding Scale
(Insert percentage here)

.... % (in no case, however, less than 10%) of the wholesale selling price of the first 200,000 copies or less; plus

.... % (in no case, however, less than 12%) of the wholesale selling price of copies in excess of 200,000 and not exceeding 500,000; plus

.... % (in no case, however, less than 15%) of the wholesale selling price of copies in excess of 500,000.

Foreign Royalties
(Insert percentage here)

(c) .... % (in no case, however, less than 50%) of all net sums received by the Publisher in respect of regular piano copies, orchestrations, band arrangements, octavos, quartets, arrangements for combinations of voices and/or instruments, and/or other copies of the composition sold in any country other than the United States and Canada, provided, however, that if the Publisher should sell such copies through, or cause them to be sold by, a subsidiary or affiliate which is actually doing business in a foreign country, then in respect of such sales, the Publisher shall pay to the Writer not less than 5% of the marked retail selling price in respect of each such copy sold and paid for.

Orchestrations and
Other Arrangements,
etc.

(d) In respect of each copy sold and paid for in the United States and Canada, or for export from the United States, of orchestrations, band arrangements, octavos, quartets, arrangements for combinations of voices and/or instruments, and/or other copies of the composition (other than regular piano copies) the following royalties on the wholesale selling price (after trade discounts, if any):

(Insert percentage here)

.... % (in no case, however, less than 10%) on the first 200,000 copies or less; plus

.... % (in no case, however, less than 12%) on all copies in excess of 200,000 and not exceeding 500,000; plus

.... % (in no case, however, less than 15%) on all copies in excess of 500,000.

Publisher's
Song Book,
Folio, etc.

(e) (i) If the composition, or any part thereof, is included in any song book, folio or similar publication issued by the Publisher containing at least four, but not more than twenty-five musical compositions, the royalty to be paid by the Publisher to the Writer shall be an amount determined by dividing 10% of the wholesale selling price (after trade discounts, if any) of the copies sold, among the total number of the Publisher's copyrighted musical compositions included in such publication. If such publication contains more than twenty-five musical compositions, the said 10% shall be increased by an additional ½% for each additional musical composition.

Licensee's
Song Book,
Folio, etc.

(ii) If, pursuant to a license granted by the Publisher to a licensee not controlled by or affiliated with it, the composition, or any part thereof, is included in any song book, folio or similar publication, containing at least four musical compositions, the royalty to be paid by the Publisher to the Writer shall be that proportion of 50% of the gross amount received by it from the licensee, as the number of uses of the composition under the license and during the license period, bears to the total number of uses of the Publisher's copyrighted musical compositions under the license and during the license period.

(iii) In computing the number of the Publisher's copyrighted musical compositions under subdivisions (i) and (ii) hereof, there shall be excluded musical compositions in the public domain and arrangements thereof and those with respect to which the Publisher does not currently publish and offer for sale regular piano copies.

(iv) Royalties on publications containing less than four musical compositions shall be payable at regular piano copy rates.

Professional Material and Free Copies	(f)	As to ''professional material'' not sold or resold, no royalty shall be payable. Free copies of the lyrics of the composition shall not be distributed except under the following conditions: (i) with the Writer's written consent; or (ii) when printed without music in limited numbers for charitable, religious or governmental purposes, or for similar public purposes, if no profit is derived, directly or indirectly; or (iii) when authorized for printing in a book, magazine or periodical, where such use is incidental to a novel or story (as distinguished from use in a book of lyrics or a lyric magazine or folio), provided that any such use shall bear the Writer's name and the proper copyright notice; or (iv) when distributed solely for the purpose of exploiting the composition, provided, that such exploitation is restricted to the distribution of limited numbers of such copies for the purpose of influencing the sale of the composition, that the distribution is independent of the sale of any other musical compositions, services, goods, wares or merchandise, and that no profit is made, directly or indirectly, in connection therewith.
Mechanicals, Electrical Transcription, Synchronization, All Other Rights	(g) **(Insert percentage here)**	..........% (in no case, however, less than 50%) of:
		All gross receipts of the Publisher in respect of any licenses (including statutory royalties) authorizing the manufacture of parts of instruments serving to mechanically reproduce the composition, or to use the composition in synchronization with sound motion pictures, or to reproduce it upon electrical transcription for broadcasting purposes; and of any and all gross receipts of the Publisher from any other source or right now known or which may hereafter come into existence, except as provided in paragraph 2.
Licensing Agent's Charges	(h)	If the Publisher administers licenses authorizing the manufacture of parts of instruments serving to mechanically reproduce said composition, or the use of said composition in synchronization or in timed relation with sound motion pictures or its reproduction upon electrical transcriptions, or any of them, through an agent, trustee or other administrator acting for a substantial part of the industry and not under the exclusive control of the Publisher (hereinafter sometimes referred to as licensing agent), the Publisher, in determining his receipts, shall be entitled to deduct from gross license fees paid by the Licensees, a sum equal to the charges paid by the Publisher to said licensing agent, provided, however, that in respect to synchronization or timed relation with sound motion pictures, said deduction shall in no event exceed $150.00 or 10% of said gross license fee, whichever is less; in connection with the manufacture of parts of instruments serving to mechanically reproduce said composition, said deductions shall not exceed 5% of said gross license fee; and in connection with electrical transcriptions, said deduction shall not exceed 10% of said gross license fee.
Block Licenses	(i)	The Publisher agrees that the use of the composition will not be included in any bulk or block license heretofore or hereafter granted, and that it will not grant any bulk or block license to include the same, without the written consent of the Writer in each instance, except (i) that the Publisher may grant such licenses with respect to electrical transcription for broadcasting purposes, but in such event, the Publisher shall pay to the Writer that proportion of 50% of the gross amount received by it under each such license as the number of uses of the composition under each such license during each such license period bears to the total number of uses of the Publisher's copyrighted musical compositions under each such license during each such license period; in computing the number of the Publisher's copyrighted musical compositions for this purpose, there shall be excluded musical compositions in the public domain and arrangements thereof and those with respect to which the Publisher does not currently publish and offer for sale regular piano copies; (ii) that the Publisher may appoint agents or representatives in countries outside of the United States and Canada to use and to grant licenses for the use of the composition on the customary royalty fee basis under which the Publisher shall receive not less than 10% of the marked retail selling price in respect of regular piano copies, and 50% of all other revenue; if, in connection with any such bulk or block license, the Publisher shall have received any advance, the Writer shall not be entitled to share therein, but no part of said advance shall be deducted in computing the composition's earnings under said bulk or block license. A bulk or block license shall be deemed to mean any license or agreement, domestic or foreign, whereby rights are granted in respect of two or more musical compositions.
Television and New Uses	(j)	Except to the extent that the Publisher and Writer have heretofore or may hereafter assign to or vest in the small performing rights licensing organization with which Writer and Publisher are affiliated, the said rights or the right to grant licenses therefor, it is agreed that no licenses shall be granted without the written consent, in each instance, of the Writer for the use of the composition by means of television, or by any means, or for any purposes not commercially established, or for which licenses were not granted by the Publisher on musical compositions prior to June 1, 1937.
Writer's Consent to Licenses	(k)	The Publisher shall not, without the written consent of the Writer in each case, give or grant any right or license (i) to use the title of the composition, or (ii) for the exclusive use of the composition in any form or for any purpose, or for any period of time, or for any territory, other than its customary arrangements with foreign publishers, or (iii) to give a dramatic representation of the composition or to dramatize the plot or story thereof, or (iv) for a vocal rendition of the composition in synchronization with sound motion pictures, or (v) for any synchronization use thereof, or (vi) for the use of the composition or a quotation or excerpt therefrom in any article, book, periodical, advertisement or other similar publication. If, however, the Publisher shall give to the Writer written notice by certified mail, return receipt requested, or telegram, specifying the right or license to be given or granted, the name of the licensee and the terms and conditions thereof, including the price or other compensation to be received therefor, then, unless the Writer (or any one or more of them) shall, within five business days after the delivery of such notice to the address of the Writer hereinafter designated, object thereto, the Publisher may grant such right or license in accordance with the said notice without first obtaining the consent of the Writer. Such notice shall be deemed sufficient if sent to the Writer at the address or addresses hereinafter designated or at the address or addresses last furnished to the Publisher in writing by the Writer.
Trust for Writer	(l)	Any portion of the receipts which may become due to the Writer from license fees (in excess of offsets), whether received directly from the licensee or from any licensing agent of the Publisher, shall, if not paid immediately on the receipt thereof by the Publisher, belong to the Writer and shall be held in trust for the Writer until payment is made; the ownership of said trust fund by the Writer shall not be questioned whether the monies are physically segregated or not.
Writer Participation	(m)	The Publisher agrees that it will not issue any license as a result of which it will receive any financial benefit in which the Writer does not participate.
Writer Credit	(n)	On all regular piano copies, orchestrations, band or other arrangements, octavos, quartets, commercial sound recordings and other reproductions of the composition or parts thereof, in whatever form and however produced, Publisher shall include or cause to be included, in addition to the copyright notice, the name of the Writer, and Publisher shall include a similar requirement in every license or authorization issued by it with respect to the composition.

126

Writers'
Respective
Shares

5. Whenever the term "Writer" is used herein, it shall be deemed to mean all of the persons herein defined as "Writer" and any and all royalties herein provided to be paid to the Writer shall be paid equally to such persons if there be more than one, unless otherwise provided in Paragraph 23.

Release of
Commercial Sound
Recording
**(Insert period not
exceeding 12 months)**

6. (a) (i) The Publisher shall, within....................months from the date of this contract (the "initial period"), cause a commercial sound recording of the composition to be made and released in the customary form and through the customary commercial channels. If at the end of such initial period a sound recording has not been made and released, as above provided, then, subject to the provisions of the next succeeding subdivision, this contract shall terminate.

**(Insert amount to be not
less than $250)**
**(Insert period not
exceeding six months)**

(ii) If, prior to the expiration of the initial period, Publisher pays the Writer the sum of $........(which shall not be charged against or recoupable out of any advances, royalties or other monies theretofor paid, then due, or which thereafter may become due the Writer from the Publisher pursuant to this contract or otherwise), Publisher shall have an additional...........months (the "additional period") commencing with the end of the initial period, within which to cause such commercial sound recording to be made and released as provided in subdivision (i) above. If at the end of the additional period a commercial sound recording has not been made and released, as above provided, then this contract shall terminate.

(iii) Upon termination pursuant to this Paragraph 6(a), all rights of any and every nature in and to the composition and in and to any and all copyrights secured thereon in the United States and throughout the world shall automatically re-vest in and become the property of the Writer and shall be reassigned to him by the Publisher. The Writer shall not be obligated to return or pay to the Publisher any advance or indebtedness as a condition of such re-assignment; the said re-assignment shall be in accordance with and subject to the provisions of Paragraph 8 hereof, and, in addition, the Publisher shall pay to the Writer all gross sums which it has theretofore or may thereafter receive in respect of the composition.

Writer's
Copies

(b) The Publisher shall furnish, or cause to be furnished, to the Writer six copies of the commercial sound recording referred to in Paragraph 6(a).

Piano Copies,
Piano Arrange-
ment or Lead Sheet
**(Select (i)
or (ii)**

(c) The Publisher shall
☐ (i) within 30 days after the initial release of a commercial sound recording of the composition, make, publish and offer for sale regular piano copies of the composition in the form and through the channels customarily employed by it for that purpose;
☐ (ii) within 30 days after execution of this contract make a piano arrangement or lead sheet of the composition and furnish six copies thereof to the Writer.

In the event neither subdivision (i) nor (ii) of this subparagraph (c) is selected, the provisions of subdivision (ii) shall be automatically deemed to have been selected by the parties.

Foreign
Copyright

7. (a) Each copyright on the composition in countries other than the United States shall be secured only in the name of the Publisher, and the Publisher shall not at any time divest itself of said foreign copyright directly or indirectly.

Foreign
Publication

(b) No rights shall be granted by the Publisher in the composition to any foreign publisher or licensee inconsistent with the terms hereof, nor shall any foreign publication rights in the composition be given to a foreign publisher or licensee unless and until the Publisher shall have complied with the provisions of Paragraph 6 hereof.

Foreign
Advance

(c) If foreign rights in the composition are separately conveyed, otherwise than as a part of the Publisher's current and/or future catalog, not less than 50% of any advance received in respect thereof shall be credited to the account of and paid to the Writer.

Foreign
Percentage

(d) The percentage of the Writer on monies received from foreign sources shall be computed on the Publisher's net receipts, provided, however, that no deductions shall be made for offsets of monies due from the Publisher to said foreign sources; or for advances made by such foreign sources to the Publisher, unless the Writer shall have received at least 50% of said advances.

No Foreign
Allocations

(e) In computing the receipts of the Publisher from licenses granted in respect of synchronization with sound motion pictures, or in respect of any world-wide licenses, or in respect of licenses granted by the Publisher for use of the composition in countries other than the United States, no amount shall be deducted for payments or allocations to publishers or licensees in such countries.

Termination
or Expiration
of Contract

8. Upon the termination or expiration of this contract, all rights of any and every nature in and to the composition and in and to any and all copyrights secured thereon in the United States and throughout the world, shall re-vest in and become the property of the Writer, and shall be re-assigned to the Writer by the Publisher free of any and all encumbrances of any nature whatsoever, provided that:

(a) If the Publisher, prior to such termination or expiration, shall have granted a domestic license for the use of the composition, not inconsistent with the terms and provisions of this contract, the re-assignment may be subject to the terms of such license.

(b) Publisher shall assign to the Writer all rights which it may have under any such agreement or license referred to in subdivision (a) in respect of the composition, including, but not limited to, the right to receive all royalties or other monies earned by the composition thereunder after the date of termination or expiration of this contract. Should the Publisher thereafter receive or be credited with any royalties or other monies so earned, it shall pay the same to the Writer.

(c) The Writer shall not be obligated to return or pay to the Publisher any advance or indebtedness as a condition of the re-assignment provided for in this Paragraph 8, and shall be entitled to receive the plates and copies of the composition in the possession of the Publisher.

(d) Publisher shall pay any and all royalties which may have accrued to the Writer prior to such termination or expiration.

(e) The Publisher shall execute any and all documents and do any and all acts or things necessary to effect any and all re-assignments to the Writer herein provided for.

Negotiations
for New or
Unspecified
Uses

9. If the Publisher desires to exercise a right in and to the composition now known or which may hereafter become known, but for which no specific provision has been made herein, the Publisher shall give written notice to the Writer thereof. Negotiations respecting all the terms and conditions of any such disposition shall thereupon be entered into between the Publisher and the Writer and no such right shall be exercised until specific agreement has been made.

Royalty Statements and Payments

10. The Publisher shall render to the Writer, hereafter, royalty statements accompanied by remittance of the amount due at the times such statements and remittances are customarily rendered by the Publisher, provided, however, that such statements and remittances shall be rendered either semi-annually or quarterly and not more than forty-five days after the end of each such semi-annual or quarterly period, as the case may be. The Writer may at any time, or from time to time, make written request for a detailed royalty statement, and the Publisher shall, within sixty days, comply therewith. Such royalty statements shall set forth in detail the various items, foreign and domestic, for which royalties are payable thereunder and the amounts thereof, including, but not limited to, the number of copies sold and the number of uses made in each royalty category. If a use is made in a publication of the character provided in Paragraph 4, subdivision (e) hereof, there shall be included in said royalty statement the title of said publication, the publisher or issuer thereof, the date of and number of uses, the gross license fee received in connection with each publication, the share thereto of all the writers under contract with the Publisher, and the Writer's share thereof. There shall likewise be included in said statement a description of every other use of the composition, and if by a licensee or licensees their name or names, and if said use is upon a part of an instrument serving to reproduce the composition mechanically, the type of mechanical reproduction, the title of the label thereon, the name or names of the artists performing the same, together with the gross license fees received, and the Writer's share thereof.

Examination of Books

11. (a) The Publisher shall from time to time, upon written demand of the Writer or his representative, permit the Writer or his representative to inspect at the place of business of the Publisher, all books, records and documents relating to the composition and all licenses granted, uses had and payments made therefor, such right of inspection to include, but not by way of limitation, the right to examine all original accountings and records relating to uses and payments by manufacturers of commercial sound recordings and music rolls; and the Writer or his representative may appoint an accountant who shall at any time during usual business hours have access to all records of the Publisher relating to the composition for the purpose of verifying royalty statements rendered or which are delinquent under the terms hereof.

(b) The Publisher shall, upon written demand of the Writer or his representative, cause any licensing agent in the United States and Canada to furnish to the Writer or his representative, statements showing in detail all licenses granted, uses had and payments made in connection with the composition, which licenses or permits were granted, or payments were received, by or through said licensing agent, and to permit the Writer or his representative to inspect at the place of business of such licensing agent, all books, records and documents of such licensing agent, relating thereto. Any and all agreements made by the Publisher with any such licensing agent shall provide that any such licensing agent will comply with the terms and provisions hereof. In the event that the Publisher shall instruct such licensing agent to furnish to the Writer or his representative statements as provided for herein, and to permit the inspection of the books, records and documents as herein provided, then if such licensing agent should refuse to comply with the said instructions, or any of them, the Publisher agrees to institute and prosecute diligently and in good faith such action or proceedings as may be necessary to compel compliance with the said instructions.

(c) With respect to foreign licensing agents, the Publisher shall make available the books or records of said licensing agents in countries outside of the United States and Canada to the extent such books or records are available to the Publisher, except that the Publisher may in lieu thereof make available any accountants' reports and audits which the Publisher is able to obtain.

(d) If as a result of any examination of books, records or documents pursuant to Paragraphs 11(a), 11(b) or 11(c) hereof, it is determined that, with respect to any royalty statement rendered by or on behalf of the Publisher to the Writer, the Writer is owed a sum equal to or greater than five percent of the sum shown on that royalty statement as being due to the Writer, then the Publisher shall pay to the Writer the entire cost of such examination, not to exceed 50% of the amount shown to be due the Writer.

(e) (i) In the event the Publisher administers its own licenses for the manufacture of parts of instruments serving to mechanically reproduce the composition rather than employing a licensing agent for that purpose, the Publisher shall include in each license agreement a provision permitting the Publisher, the Writer or their respective representatives to inspect, at the place of business of such licensee, all books, records and documents of such licensee relating to such license. Within 30 days after written demand by the Writer, the Publisher shall commence to inspect such licensee's books, records and documents and shall furnish a written report of such inspection to the Writer within 90 days following such demand. If the Publisher fails, after written demand by the Writer, to so inspect the licensee's books, records and documents, or fails to furnish such report, the Writer or his representative may inspect such licensee's books, records and documents at his own expense.

(ii) In the further event that the Publisher and the licensee referred to in subdivision (i) above are subsidiaries or affiliates of the same entity or one is a subsidiary or affiliate of the other, then, unless the Publisher employs a licensing agent to administer the licenses referred to in subdivision (i) above, the Writer shall have the right to make the inspection referred to in subdivision (i) above without the necessity of making written demand on the Publisher as provided in subdivision (i) above.

(iii) If as a result of any inspection by the Writer pursuant to subdivisions (i) and (ii) of this subparagraph (e) the Writer recovers additional monies from the licensee, the Publisher and the Writer shall share equally in the cost of such inspection.

Default in Payment or Prevention of Examination

12. If the Publisher shall fail or refuse, within sixty days after written demand, to furnish or cause to be furnished, such statements, books, records or documents, or to permit inspection thereof, as provided for in Paragraphs 10 and 11 hereof, or within thirty days after written demand, to make the payment of any royalties due under this contract, then the Writer shall be entitled, upon ten days' written notice, to terminate this contract. However if the Publisher shall:

(a) Within the said ten-day period serve upon the Writer a written notice demanding arbitration; and

(b) Submit to arbitration its claim that it has complied with its obligation to furnish statements, books, records or documents, or permitted inspection thereof or to pay royalties, as the case may be, or both, and thereafter comply with any award of the arbitrator within ten days after such award or within such time as the arbitrator may specify;

then this contract shall continue in full force and effect as if the Writer had not sent such notice of termination. If the Publisher shall fail to comply with the foregoing provisions, then this contract shall be deemed to have been terminated as of the date of the Writer's written notice of termination.

Derivative Works

13. No derivative work prepared under authority of Publisher during the term of this contract may be utilized by Publisher or any other party after termination or expiration of this contract.

Notices

14. All written demands and notices provided for herein shall be sent by certified mail, return receipt requested.

Suits for Infringement

15. Any legal action brought by the Publisher against any alleged infringer of the composition shall be initiated and prosecuted at its sole cost and expense, but if the Publisher should fail, within thirty days after written demand, to institute such action, the Writer shall be entitled to institute such suit at his cost and expense. All sums recovered as a result of any such action shall, after the deduction of the reasonable expense thereof, be divided equally between the Publisher and the Writer. No settlement of any such action may be made by either party without first notifying the other; in the event that either party should object to such settlement, then such settlement shall not be made if the party objecting assumes the prosecution of the action and all expenses thereof, except that any sums thereafter recovered shall be divided equally between the Publisher and the Writer after the deduction of the reasonable expenses thereof.

Infringement Claims

16. (a) If a claim is presented against the Publisher alleging that the composition is an infringement upon some other work or a violation of any other right of another, and because therof the Publisher is jeopardized, it shall forthwith serve a written notice upon the Writer setting forth the full details of such claim. The pendency of said claim shall not relieve the Publisher of the obligation to make payment of the royalties to the Writer hereunder, unless the Publisher shall deposit said royalties as and when they would otherwise be payable, in an account in the joint names of the Publisher and the Writer in a bank or trust company in New York, New York, if the Writer on the date of execution of this contract resides East of the Mississippi River, or in Los Angeles, California, if the Writer on the date of execution of this contract resides West of the Mississippi River. If no suit be filed within nine months after said written notice from the Publisher to the Writer, all monies deposited in said joint account shall be paid over to the Writer plus any interest which may have been earned thereon.

(b) Should an action be instituted against the Publisher claiming that the composition is an infringement upon some other work or a violation of any other right of another, the Publisher shall forthwith serve written notice upon the Writer containing the full details of such claim. Notwithstanding the commencement of such action, the Publisher shall continue to pay the royalties hereunder to the Writer unless it shall, from and after the date of the service of the summons, deposit said royalties as and when they would otherwise be payable, in an account in the joint names of the Publisher and the Writer in a bank or trust company in New York, New York, if the Writer on the date of execution of this contract resides East of the Mississippi River, or in Los Angeles, California, if the Writer on the date of execution of this contract resides West of the Mississippi River. If the said suit shall be finally adjudicated in favor of the Publisher or shall be settled, there shall be released and paid to the Writer all of such sums held in escrow less any amount paid out of the Writer's share with the Writer's written consent in settlement of said action. Should the said suit finally result adversely to the Publisher, the said amount on deposit shall be released to the Publisher to the extent of any expense or damage it incurs and the balance shall be paid over to the Writer.

(c) In any of the foregoing events, however, the Writer shall be entitled to payment of said royalties or the money so deposited at and after such time as he files with the Publisher a surety company bond, or a bond in other form acceptable to the Publisher, in the sum of such payments to secure the return thereof to the extent that the Publisher may be entitled to such return. The foregoing payments or deposits or the filing of a bond shall be without prejudice to the rights of the Publisher or Writer in the premises.

Arbitration

17. Any and all differences, disputes or controversies arising out of or in connection with this contract shall be submitted to arbitration before a sole arbitrator under the then prevailing rules of the American Arbitration Association. The location of the arbitration shall be New York, New York, if the Writer on the date of execution of this contract resides East of the Mississippi River, or Los Angeles, California, if the Writer on the date of execution of this contract resides West of the Mississippi River. The parties hereby individually and jointly agree to abide by and perform any award rendered in such arbitration. Judgment upon any such award rendered may be entered in any court having jurisdiction thereof.

Assignment

18. Except to the extent herein otherwise expressly provided, the Publisher shall not sell, transfer, assign, convey, encumber or otherwise dispose of the composition or the copyright or copyrights secured thereon without the prior written consent of the Writer. The Writer has been induced to enter into this contract in reliance upon the value to him of the personal service and ability of the Publisher in the exploitation of the composition, and by reason thereof it is the intention of the parties and the essence of the relationship between them that the rights herein granted to the Publisher shall remain with the Publisher and that the same shall not pass to any other person, including, without limitations, successors to or receivers or trustees of the property of the Publisher, either by act or deed of the Publisher or by operation of law, and in the event of the voluntary or involuntary bankruptcy of the Publisher, this contract shall terminate, provided, however, that the composition may be included by the Publisher in a bona fide voluntary sale of its music business or its entire catalog of musical compositions, or in a merger or consolidation of the Publisher with another corporation, in which event the Publisher shall immediately give written notice thereof to the Writer; and provided further that the composition and the copyright therein may be assigned by the Publisher to a subsidiary or affiliated company generally engaged in the music publishing business. If the Publisher is an individual, the composition may pass to a legatee or distributee as part of the inheritance of the Publisher's music business and entire catalog of musical compositions. Any such transfer or assignment shall, however, be conditioned upon the execution and delivery by the transferee or assignee to the Writer of an agreement to be bound by and to perform all of the terms and conditions of this contract to be performed on the part of the Publisher.

Subsidiary Defined

19. A subsidiary, affiliate, or any person, firm or corporation controlled by the Publisher or by such subsidiary or affiliate, as used in this contract, shall be deemed to include any person, firm or corporation, under common control with, or the majority of whose stock or capital contribution is owned or controlled by the Publisher or by any of its officers, directors, partners or associates, or whose policies and actions are subject to domination or control by the Publisher or any of its officers, directors, partners or associates.

Amounts

20. The amounts and percentages specified in this contract shall be deemed to be the amounts and percentages agreed upon by the parties hereto, unless other amounts or percentages are inserted in the blank spaces provided therefor.

Modifications

21. This contract is binding upon and shall enure to the benefit of the parties hereto and their respective successors in interest (as hereinbefore limited). If the Writer (or one or more of them) shall not be living, any notices may be given to, or consents given by, his or their successors in interest. No change or modification of this contract shall be effective unless reduced to writing and signed by the parties hereto.

The words in this contract shall be so construed that the singular shall include the plural and the plural shall include the singular where the context so requires and the masculine shall include the feminine and the feminine shall include the masculine where the context so requires.

Paragraph Headings

22. The paragraph headings are inserted only as a matter of convenience and for reference, and in no way define, limit or describe the scope or intent of this contract nor in any way affect this contract.

Special Provisions

23.

Used by permission of the Songwriters Guild of America.

The Songwriters Guild of America

1500 Harbor Blvd., Weehawken, NJ 07087, (201) 867-7603
6430 Sunset Blvd., Suite #1002, Hollywood, CA 90028, (213) 462-1108
1222 16th Ave. South, Nashville, TN 37212, (615) 329-1782
1560 Broadway, Suite #1306, New York, NY 10036, (212) 768-7902

Overview — SGA Popular Songwriters Contact

The **Songwriters Guild of America** is a voluntary association of songwriters; it is not a union. The SGA Contract, (the "Contract") is thus not a negotiated contract between publishers and the Guild. Rather, the Contract has been prepared by SGA and it's counsel and represents what the Guild believes to be the best minimum songwriter contract available.

The Contract is an agreement between a songwriter (or co-writers) and his/her publisher, and sets forth their respective rights and obligations with respect to a song or songs.

In order to facilitate a general understanding of the terms of the Contract, the following is a brief summary of its highlights.

Paragraph 1

Writer assigns his/her song to the Publisher throughout the world for a designated number of years, not to exceed forty (40) or thirty-five (35) years from the date of first release of a commercial sound recording. (The term reflects the provisions of the 1976 Copyright Revision Law.) The shorter the term, the better for the Writer because if the song is successful, he/she can renegotiate more favorable financial terms at an earlier time. The length of the term would depend on the bargaining strength and reputation of the Writer.

Paragraph 2

This recognizes that the Writer is a member of a particular performing rights society (either ASCAP, BMI, or SESAC) and that this Contract will not interfere with the Writer's collection of performing rights proceeds directly from his/her performing rights society. It is crucial that the Writer and Publisher are members of the same performing rights society.

Paragraph 3

Writer warrants that the song was written by him/her, is original, and that the Writer has the right to enter into the agreement.

Paragraph 4

Sets forth royalties to be paid for various types of uses of the song. Note that the Contract sets forth *minimum* amounts that the Writer must receive. Of course, the Writer is free to attempt to negotiate for higher royalty rates. If no amounts are filled in, the minimum amounts apply (see Paragarph 20 of the initial contract). Paragraph 4(k) provides that the initial publisher may not, without the Writer's written consent, grant certain licenses not specifically permitted by the contract (e.g. use of the title of the song; to give a dramatic representation of the song; synchonization, licenses, etc.)

Paragraph 5

This applies if there is more than on Writer. If so, each Writer will share royalties equally, unless specified otherwise in Paragraph 23.

Paragraph 6

This requires the Publisher to have a commercial sound recording of the song made and released within twelve (12) months from the date of the Contract or to pay Writer a sum of not less that Two Hundred and Fifty ($250.00) dollars for the right to extend this period of not more than six (6) months. If the Publisher does not comply, the Contract terminates and all rights return to Writer. When the sound recording is cut, the Publisher is required to give the Writer six (6) copies of the sound recording.

Under Paragraph 6(c), the Publisher must either (i) publish and offer for sale regular piano copies of the song within thirty (30) days of release of the sound recording; or (ii) make a piano arrangement or lead sheet of the song within thirty (30) day of execution of the Contract (with six (6) copies to be given to the Writer). The parties must select which of the above alternatives will apply.

Paragraph 7

Deals with the Publisher's sublicensing of the song in foreign countries. It guarantees that the Writer will receive no less than 50% of the revenue by the Publisher from rights licensed outside the U.S.

Paragraph 8

Explains what happens when the Contract terminates (i.e., all rights revert to the Writer, subject to any outstanding licenses issued by the Publisher and the latter's duty to account for monies received after termination.

Paragraph 9

Deals with exploitation of the song in a manner not yet contemplated and thus not specifically covered in the Contract. Any such exploitation must be mutually agreed upon by the Writer and the Publisher.

Paragraph 10, 11 & 12

Deals with the method of payment of royalties to the Writer and the Writer's right to inspect Publisher's books.

Paragraph 13

Various uses of the song, such as sound recordings and arrangements, are considered "derivative works" under the Copyright Law. Often, such derivative works can have more financial value than the original sheet music. This provision provides that when the contract terminates, the Publisher loses all rights in such derivative works, as well as in the original version of the song.

Paragraph 15 & 16

Deals with bringing lawsuits against infringers and defending lawsuits in the event someone claims that the Writer's song infringed a copyright

Paragraph 17

In the event there is a dispute between the Writer and the Publisher and they cannot resolve it, such dispute is to be settled by arbitration (generally considered a more expeditious and inexpensive means of settling claims).

Paragraph 18

This places restrictions on Publisher's rights to sell the Writer's song to another publisher other than as a part of the Publisher's entire catalog.

MECHANICAL LICENSE

To: [Record Company]   Date:

Refer to provisions of this agreement listed below, which vary the terms of the compulsory license provision of the Copyright Act. The following is supplementary thereto:

 1. Song Title:

 2. Publisher:

 3. Phonorecord No.:

 4. Artist:

 5. Album Title:

 6. Royalty Rate:

 7. Date of Release:

This Agreement is limited to the United States, its territories and possessions.

You have advised us that you wish to obtain a compulsory license to make and distribute phonorecords of the copyrighted work referred to herein, under the compulsory license provision of Section 115 of the Copyright Act.

Upon your doing so, you shall have all the rights which are granted to, and all obligations which are imposed upon, users of said copyrighted work under the compulsory license provision of the Copyright Act, after phonorecords of the copyrighted work have been distributed to the public in the United States under the authority of the copyright owner by another person, except that with respect to phonorecords thereof made and distributed hereunder:

1. You shall pay royalties and account to us quarterly, within forty-five (45) days after the end of each calendar quarter, on the basis of net phonorecords made and distributed;

2. For such phonorecords made and distributed, the royalty shall be the rate stated above;

3. This compulsory license covers and is limited to one particular recording of said copyrighted work as performed by the artist and on the phonorecord number identified above; and this compulsory license does not supersede nor in any way affect any prior agreements now in effect respecting phonorecords of said copyrighted work;

4. Proper writer and publisher credit (i.e., the name[s] of the writer[s] and publisher[s] of said copyrighted work) shall be included on each and every copy of all such phonorecords covered by this license.

5. In the event you fail to account to us and pay royalties as herein provided for, we may give written notice to you that, unless the default is remedied within thirty (30) days of your receipt of the notice, this compulsory license will be automatically terminated. Such termination shall render either the making or the distribution, or both, of all phonorecords for which royalties have not been paid, actionable as acts of infringement under, and fully subject to the remedies provided by, the Copyright Act.

6. You need not serve or file the notice of intention to obtain a compulsory license required by the Copyright Act.

7. We or our designees shall have the right to audit your books and records with respect to statements rendered pursuant to this license during regular business hours at your office.

Very Truly Yours,

By: _____
    Publisher

We acknowledge the receipt of a copy hereof and the accuracy of the terms contained herein;

By: _____
    Record Company

RECOMMENDED READING

Brabec, Jeffrey, and Todd Brabec. *Music, Money and Success*. New York, NY: Schirmer Books, 1994.

Braheny, John. *The Craft & Business of Songwriting*. Cincinnati, OH: Writer's Digest Books, 1987.

Cahn, Sammy. *The Songwriter's Rhyming Dictionary*. New York, NY: New American Library, 1984.

Davis, Sheila. *The Craft of Lyric Writing*. Cincinnati, OH: Writer's Digest Books, 1985.

Davis, Sheila. *Successful Lyric Writing*. Cincinnati, OH: Writer's Digest Books, 1987.

Halloran, Esq., Mark, Editor. *The Musician's Business and Legal Guide*. NJ: Prentice Hall, 1991.

Jasen, David A. *Tin Pan Alley: the Composers, the Songs, the Performers & Their Times: The Golden Age of American Popular Music from 1886 to 1956*. New York, NY: D. I. Fine, 1988.

Kasha, Al, and Joel Hirschhorn. *If They Ask You, You Can Write a Song*. New York, NY: Simon and Schuster, 1979.

Martin, George, ed. *Making Music—The Guide to Writing, Recording & Performing*. New York, NY: Morrow, 1983.

Monaco, Bob and James Riordan. *The Platinum Rainbow; How to Succeed in the Music Business Without Selling Your Soul*. Chicago, IL: Contemporary Books, 1988.

Rachlin, Harvey. *The Songwriter's & Musician's Guide to Making Great Demos*. Cincinnati, OH: Writer's Digest Books, 1988.

Rapaport, Diane Sward. *How to Make & Sell Your Own Record*. Jerome, AZ: Jerome Headlands, 1987.

Siegel, Alan H. *Breakin' in . . . to the Music Business*. Port Chester, NY: Cherry Lane, 1986.

Songwriter's Market (Annual). Cincinnati, OH: Writer's Digest Books.

Williams, George. *The Songwriter's Demo Manual and Success Guide*. Bridgeport, CA: Music Business Books/Tree by River, 1984.

Index